Coming Next Week

A Paramount Picture

SIXTH of the "Famous 41," this will be a sensation everywhere. Can you imagine Glorious Gloria as the dancing sensation of Paris—with over a score of daring, dazzling dance costumes?

David Powell, Harrison Ford and Walter Hiers are in the cast.

A Sam Wood Production

FAMOUS PLAYERS·LASKY CORPORATION
ADOLPH ZUKOR Pres.   JESSE L. LASKY   CECIL B. DE MILLE
NEW YORK

From the play by
Ann Nichols
Scenario by
Elmer Harris and
Percy Heath.

JESSE L. LASKY
PRESENTS

GLORIA SWANSON
IN "Her Gilded Cage"

COMING NEXT WEEK

A Pictorial History of Film Advertising

RUSSELL C. SWEENEY

CASTLE BOOKS – NEW YORK

© 1973 by A. S. Barnes and Co., Inc.

HF
6161
M6
S85

Library of Congress Cataloging in Publication Data

Sweeney, Russell C
  Coming next week.

  1. Advertising—Moving-pictures—History—Pictorial works. I. Title.
HF6161.M6S85   659.1′9′79143   71-37823

This Edition Published by Arrangement with A. S. Barnes & Co., Inc.

Printed in the United States of America

Preface

On the following pages you will see a pictorial history of motion-picture newspaper and magazine advertising over a twenty-one year period.

This pictorial history covers the period from the 1920s, when most newspaper ads were plain pen-and-ink drawings, to the 1930s and 1940s, when the advancement in newsprint and the printing itself allowed for more realistic photos, or halftone printing. I have refrained from any critical analysis or social commentary, for that has been done many times, and done far better than I could hope to do.

My purpose is only to take the reader on a nostalgic journey back to the days of double features, two-reel comedies, and the exorbitant night admission price of 60¢ in the larger movie palaces.

Have fun, read the ads, and see how many times you'll see "Greater than his last picture!"

Russell Sweeney

77-101-04

PREFACE

Coming Next Week

1920

Buster Keaton was one of the most promising new comedians of the year. Six year old Jackie Coogan was making his first screen appearance with Charlie Chaplin in *The Kid*. Thomas Meighan, one of the most popular stars, maintained his hold on the public in *Civilian Clothes*. Paramount Pictures produced one of the big films of the year, *Dr. Jekyll and Mr. Hyde,* starring the distinguished stage actor John Barrymore. Mary Pickford, Douglas Fairbanks, Charlie Chaplin and D. W. Griffith formed United Artists Corporation to produce and release their pictures. Buck Jones starred in his first western for Fox Studios, *The Last Straw*.

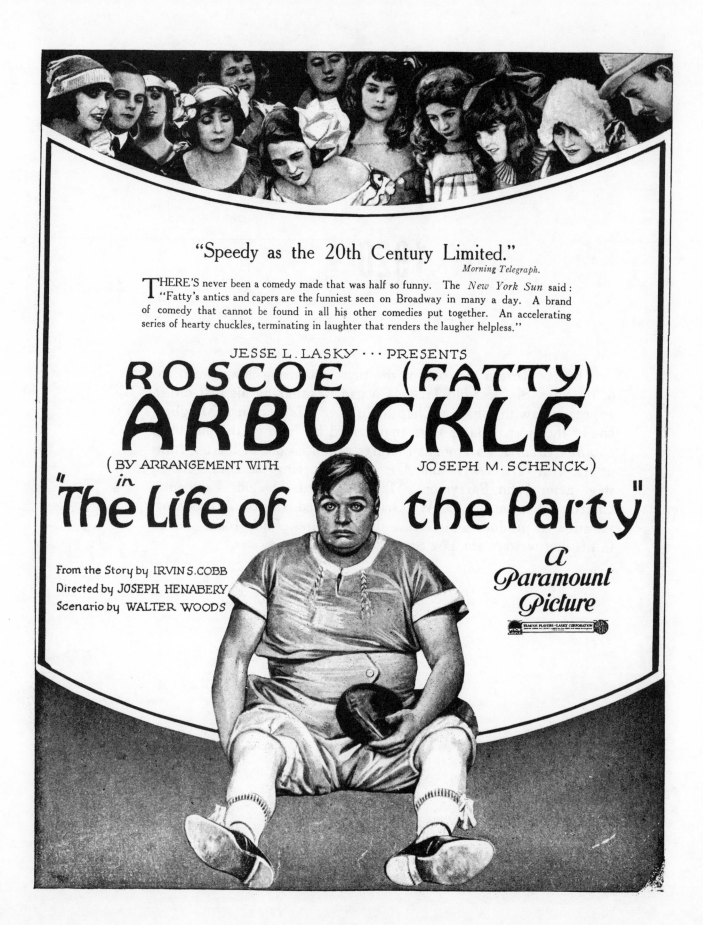

"Speedy as the 20th Century Limited."
Morning Telegraph.

THERE'S never been a comedy made that was half so funny. The *New York Sun* said: "Fatty's antics and capers are the funniest seen on Broadway in many a day. A brand of comedy that cannot be found in all his other comedies put together. An accelerating series of hearty chuckles, terminating in laughter that renders the laugher helpless."

JESSE L. LASKY ··· PRESENTS

ROSCOE (FATTY) ARBUCKLE

(BY ARRANGEMENT WITH   JOSEPH M. SCHENCK)

in "The Life of the Party"

From the Story by IRVIN S. COBB
Directed by JOSEPH HENABERY
Scenario by WALTER WOODS

A *Paramount Picture*

FAMOUS PLAYERS—LASKY CORPORATION

Adapted for the screen   by
LAMBERT HILLYER
from the story "Dan Kurrie's Inning"
BY RUSSELL A. BOGGS
Directed by LAMBERT HILLYER
Photographed by JOE AUGUST A.S.C.
A WILLIAM S. HART Production

William S. HART
in
"SAND!"

And it's a hummer! A story of the West—
with gun fights and train robberies, and thrills by
the dozen!

A Paramount Artcraft Picture

MABEL NORMAND
in
The Slim Princess

Fat! Tons and tons of it.

Bumping, wheezing, bouncing about the
harem of the ruler of Morovenia in the
shape of dozens of enormous women!

The little Princess Kalora was a violet in
a garden of peonies. But in the eyes of
the Morovenian lounge lizards she didn't
have a chance—and never would until the
day when she could boast of at least three
chins.

They Weighed Beauty by the Pound

MARY PICKFORD

comes to us at last in

"Pollyanna"

one of the great stories for which the amusement loving world has long awaited

From Eleanor H. Porter's Novel "Pollyanna"
Published by the Page Company
Screen Adaptation by Frances Marion
Photographed by Charles Rosher

"Pollyanna is the High Priestess of Optimism. She is not merely the discoverer, but the 33rd degree exploiter of the silver lining. The fairies who made sunshine from the cucumbers were insignificant beings to "Pollyanna." She is full of action, sparkle and pathos, and will help you to turn your sorrows, big or small, into gladness.

Parkway

NORTH AVE. AT CHARLES

JESSE L. LASKY *presents*
WALLACE REID
in
"DOUBLE SPEED"
A Paramount Artcraft Picture

Robbed by tramps—Thrown from a bank as a hobo—Chauffeur to the girl he loves—Impersonating his millionaire self in society—Married in secret—Accused of his own murder—These are only a few of the amazing adventures of devil-may-care "Speed" Carr.

A Picture That Sizzles Over the Screen!

With WANDA HAWLEY, THEODORE ROBERTS, TULLY MARSHALL

"WE'LL draw lots for her!" they shouted. Eight drunken men. And the girl who had played "Nelly Grey," and moved him as he had never been moved before.

"No! We'll fight for her!" And eight men crumpled beneath his thundering blows!

Then—mad and drunk and bleeding, he set out to get her!

What then? One of the tenderest love stories ever told, a story that will touch your heart like the strains of an old song.

Greater in thrills, in drama and in heart interest than any Hart picture before.

By WILLIAM S. HART
Adapted and directed by LAMBERT HILLYER
Photographed by JOE AUGUST, A.S.C.

A William S. Hart Production

FAMOUS PLAYERS–LASKY CORPORATION
ADOLPH ZUKOR Pres. JESSE L. LASKY Vice Pres. CECIL B. DE MILLE Director General
NEW YORK

William S. Hart
in
"THE TESTING BLOCK"
A Paramount Picture

Parkway
NORTH AVENUE AT CHARLES

DOROTHY GISH
in
"Little Miss Rebellion"

Fate made her a grand duchess, and palace rules and flunkeys made her sick.

So she declared herself a human being and set out to wreck traditions. Aided and abetted by a gang of baseball Yankees!

Then, bang! went a revolution, and blew her straight into love and a job in a New York beanery.

Whirls of excitement, a riot of laughs, and the funniest girl on the screen.

**Special Musical Score
Arranged by
V. Nessul, Musical Director**

A Paramount Picture

J. PARKER READ, J? PRESENTS
LOUISE GLAUM
in
SEX
C. GARDNER SULLIVAN
DIRECTED BY FRED NIBLO

MONDAY-TUESDAY-WEDNESDAY

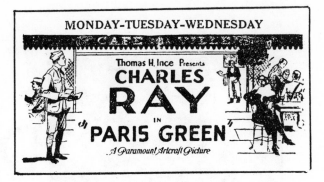

Thomas H. Ince Presents
CHARLES RAY
IN
"PARIS GREEN"
A Paramount Artcraft Picture

The First National Exhibitors' Circuit Presents
Katherine MacDonald
The American Beauty
In
"The Turning Point"

Never Was Love's
First Meeting
Under Such
Strange
Circumstances—

SHE THOUGHT HIM A BURGLAR—
HE THOUGHT HER AN INTERLOPER—

"The Mark of Zorro."

Action, romance, mystery, thrills and comedy in fullest measure—all the elements of the Fairbanks successes of the past, yet in a more picturesque and colorful setting than any release you have yet had from this idol of the masses.

DOUGLAS FAIRBANKS

in

"THE MARK OF ZORRO"

From the "All Story Weekly" Novel, "The Curse of Capistrano" by Johnston McCulley

Directed by
FRED NIBLO

UNITED ARTISTS CORPORATION
MARY PICKFORD · CHARLIE CHAPLIN · DOUGLAS FAIRBANKS · D.W.GRIFFITH
HIRAM ABRAMS, PRESIDENT

CARL LAEMMLE presents

UNDER CRIMSON SKIES

A Glorious Romance of Love and High-Seas Adventure

TRULY, a great picture. A rousing, stirring picture. A romantic picture. A story that sweeps you up out of your humdrum life and carries you off to sea—to fight with strong, silent Elmo Lincoln. against the perils of mutiny on the high seas—to fall in love with a beautiful woman and sacrifice liberty for her sake—to make a miraculous escape from the fetid dungeon of a southern republic and become master of a colony of beach-combers, conquering them by might of fist and brain and then—to save the one woman from a terrible fate in the midst of red revolution. Splendidly acted by a great company in outdoor scenes of tempest and sunshine rarely equalled for their marvelous photography. One of the few big productions of the year.

Starring
ELMO LINCOLN
Directed by REX INGRAM   Story by J. G. HAWKS
UNIVERSAL-JEWEL
SUPER-PRODUCTION

In Old Kentucky
FEATURING
ANITA STEWART

Not Just a Picture But a Great Show

GREAT CROWDS
WEPT AND CHEERED

LIONEL
BARRYMORE
"THE COPPER-
HEAD"
Exclusive Pittsburgh
presentation
at the
REGENT
ALL THIS
WEEK

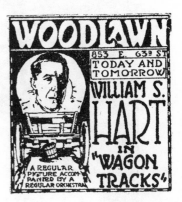

WOODLAWN
853 E. 63⁹ ST
TODAY AND
TOMORROW
WILLIAM S.
HART
IN
"WAGON
TRACKS"
A REGULAR
PICTURE ACCOM-
PANIED BY A
REGULAR ORCHESTRA

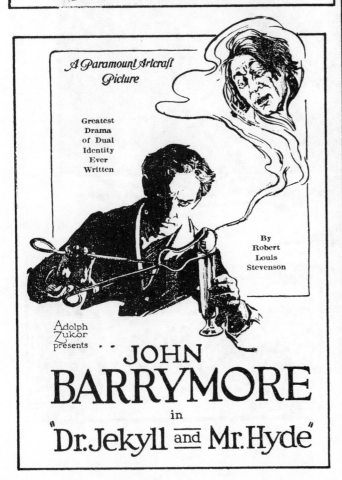

*A Paramount Artcraft
Picture*

Greatest
Drama
of Dual
Identity
Ever
Written

By
Robert
Louis
Stevenson

Adolph
Zukor
presents

JOHN
BARRYMORE
in
"Dr. Jekyll and Mr. Hyde"

Jesse L. Lasky presents
ETHEL
CLAYTON
in
"A Lady in Love"
WITH
Harrison Ford
In a Production as Close to Life as
"THE THIRTEENTH COMMANDMENT"
And as Close to the Heart as
"THE YOUNG MRS. WINTHROP"

WILLIAM FOX
presents
The new screen sensation
BUCK JONES
A four square son of the open prairies in a four square play of love and thrill-
THE LAST STRAW
by
HAROLD TITUS

Directed by
DENISON CLIFT

Jesse L. Lasky presents
WALLACE REID in "Sick Abed"
A Paramount Artcraft Picture

DOUGLAS FAIRBANKS

in

"The Mollycoddle"

Scenario by Tom Geraghty
Story by Harold McGrath.

Story value—plus—in this
newest offering of the
inimitable "Doug"—
Suspense-absorbing interest-
thrills—"he-man" action—
And comedy novelties such
as Fairbanks at his best
alone can produce.

UNITED ARTISTS CORPORATION
Mary Pickford · Charlie Chaplin · Douglas Fairbanks · D. W. Griffith
Hiram Abrams, General Manager

21

IF ITS GOOD ITS AT THE
BRIDGE
EDMONDSON AT PULASKI

Monday and Tuesday
WALLACE REID
In "HAWTHORNE OF THE U. S. A."

SEE—Hawthorne break the bank at Monte Carlo!

SEE—him shoot the blood of life into the doddering old kingdom of Bovinia and show 'em how we do things in the U.S.A!

SEE—the great supporting cast:—L'la Lee, Theodore Roberts, Harrison Ford, Tully Marshall, Charles Ogle, Edwin Stevens, Guy Oliver!

For Other Big Attractions
See Guide to Films

Thomas H. Ince presents
DOROTHY DALTON
"The Dark Mirror"
A Paramount Artcraft Picture

CHARLES RAY
IN
"A TAILOR MADE MAN"

Jesse L. Lasky presents

THOMAS MEIGHAN
in
"Civilian Clothes"

With
Beautiful
Martha Mansfield

An All-Wool Romance, Lined with Silk and Stitched Throughout with Laughter

A Paramount Picture

OVER there, in his captain's uniform, he had been her beau ideal of a man. Over here, in his butler's garb or his noisy "hand-me-downs"—well, this snobbish little aristocrat hadn't planned for that!

But he was her husband, married in France. And fighting Sam McGinnis made her fit to be called his wife in America!

From the Famous Stage Success by
THOMPSON BUCHANAN
Scenario by Clara S. Beranger

Thomas H. Ince presents
Douglas MacLean
in "Chickens"
A Paramount Picture
Funniest Film on Record

22

1921

It was a big year for Douglas Fairbanks with his exciting costume drama *The Three Musketeers*. Richard Barthelmess was appearing in his first starring role as *Tol'able David*. Mary Pickford played a dual role in *Little Lord Fauntleroy,* while Tom Mix was giving William S. Hart strong competition as leading western star of the screen. Rudolph Valentino began the best years of his career in *The Sheik,* while Wallace Reid was racing his cars as reigning king of the Paramount studios. Neighborhood theater admissions were usually 15¢ or 25¢ for a feature picture, newsreel, two-reel comedy, coming attractions, and maybe a travelogue thrown in for good measure.

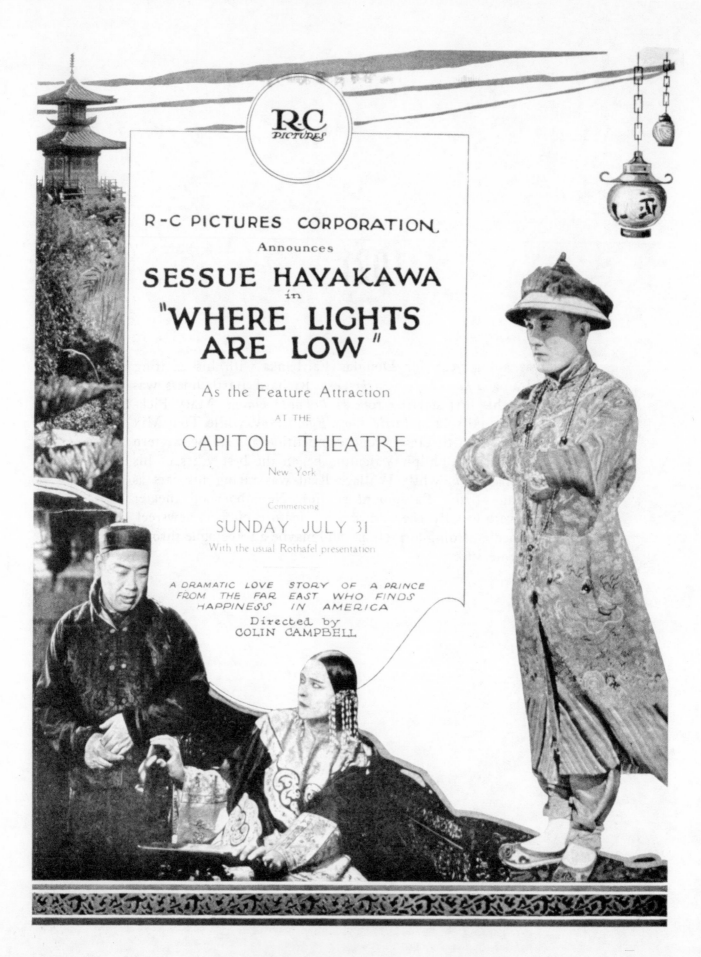

Here is the greatest

MARY PICKFORD

picture ever released

"Little Lord Fauntleroy"

A book that has delighted millions, a story that lives in the memory of all the men and women who were yesterday's children, made into a glorious film for the joy of young and old the world over

FROM FRANCES HODGSON BURNETT'S FAMOUS STORY

SCENARIO BY BERNARD McCONVILLE
PHOTOGRAPHY BY CHARLES ROSHER
DIRECTION BY JACK PICKFORD AND
ALFRED E. GREEN

UNITED
ARTISTS
CORPORATION

MARY PICKFORD
CHARLIE CHAPLIN
DOUGLAS FAIRBANKS
D. W. GRIFFITH
HIRAM ABRAMS, PRESIDENT

THE SH

A photoplay of tempestuous love between a madcap English Beauty and a bronzed Arab chief

From the novel by
EDITH M. HULL
Scenario by
MONTE M. KATTERJOHN

AGNES AYRES, who made such a wonderful success in Cecil B. de Mille's "Forbidden Fruit" and "The Affairs of Anatol"
RUDOLPH VALENTINO, whose distinguished acting in "The Four Horsemen of the Apocalypse" is remembered by millions.

It's a Paramount

Jesse L. Lasky presents a
GEORGE MELFORD
PRODUCTION
with AGNES AYRES and RUDOLPH VALENTINO

EIK

"When an Arab sees a woman he wants he takes her"
—Ancient Proverb of Arabia.

THAT was the meaning of love in the desert until The Sheik met the English girl.

That is the heart of the plot of "The Sheik," which in book form is the year's sensation on both sides of the Atlantic and which as a Paramount Picture finds and thrills a multi-million audience.

Don't miss the thrill of seeing the proud mad-cap English girl snatched from the sand by the hard-riding Sheik of a hundred tribes.

You will be amazed at her life within the tented luxury of the Sahara.

You will see love making by the handsome Rudolph Valentino as The Sheik which is in the full torrent of Oriental tradition.

How shall the lovely and aristocratic Agnes Ayres, as the English girl, escape with life and honor?

That is the plot of it, the shiver of it — the odds are so great — that is the drama you see against a background of infinite desert,

—of a thousand wild Bedouin horsemen with long rifles and flowing robes,

—of the bride-market at Biskra where the slave-brides are sold,

—and of desert fighting between Sheik and Bandit, and between their troops, of a ferocity only equalled by tigers.

Does love emerge supreme and glorious at the climax? Is a pure spot found in the heart of the bronzed Sheik?

The answer to that will make you draw the deepest breath of all,

—and recognize that once more Paramount has given you the best show in town or state.

Ask your theatre when it's coming.

FAMOUS PLAYERS~LASKY CORPORATION

Picture

FIRST SHOWING
at more than 250 leading theatres
NEXT WEEK

AN All-Arbuckle, all-comedy knockout that is funnier than "The Life of the Party."

Grab hold of some of "Brewster's Millions!"

JESSE L LASKY
PRESENTS,

ROSCOE (FATTY)

Arbuckle
(BY ARRANGEMENT WITH JOSEPH M. SCHENCK)

in "Brewster's Millions"
A Paramount Picture

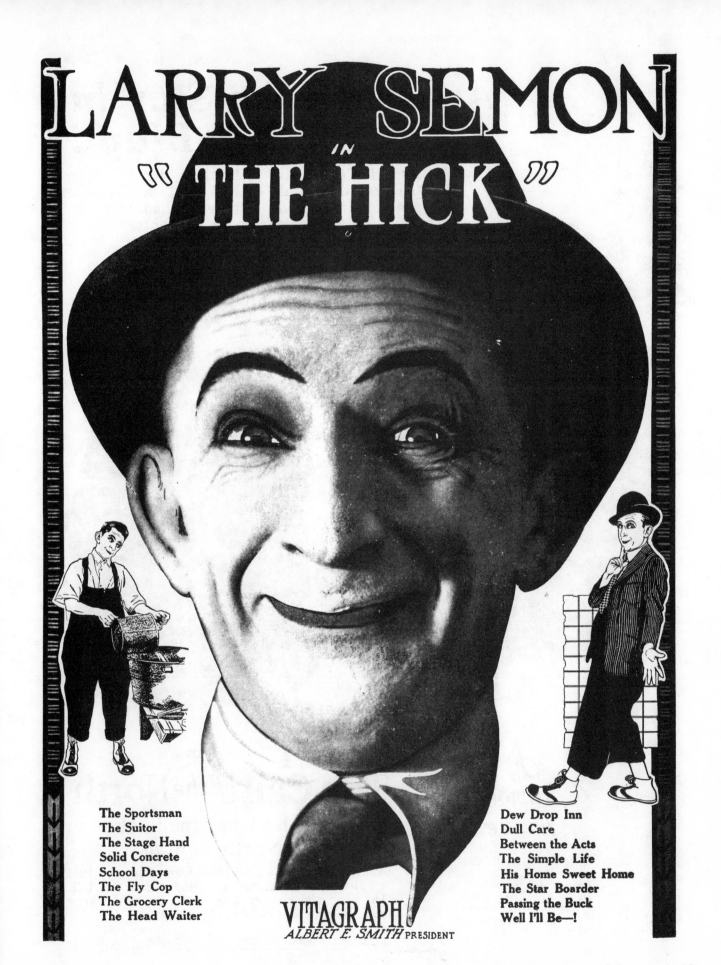

LARRY SEMON

in

"THE HICK"

The Sportsman
The Suitor
The Stage Hand
Solid Concrete
School Days
The Fly Cop
The Grocery Clerk
The Head Waiter

Dew Drop Inn
Dull Care
Between the Acts
The Simple Life
His Home Sweet Home
The Star Boarder
Passing the Buck
Well I'll Be—!

VITAGRAPH
ALBERT E. SMITH PRESIDENT

A Great New Star in a Great Big Play!

Jack Holt's first star picture! A star that represents all that is best in American manhood. A star who's had the public with him from the moment they saw him first.

A Paramount Picture

Based on the novel, "Conjuror's House," by Stewart Edward White, and the play by George Broadhurst. Scenario by John Cunningham. Directed by Joseph Henabery.

Jesse L. Lasky presents

JACK HOLT in

"The Call of the North"

The play that made the Far North famous!

A hit in the book, a hit on the stage. The play that a hundred writers tried to imitate—and couldn't. The play whose every scene has a thrill for every man, woman and child in the country.

FAMOUS PLAYERS·LASKY CORPORATION
ADOLPH ZUKOR *Pres.* JESSE L. LASKY *Vice Pres.* CECIL B. DE MILLE *Director General*
NEW YORK

William S. Hart

in

"WHITE OAK"

BY WILLIAM S. HART

"IT is the most thrilling picture in which William S. Hart has appeared in all the twenty-five years he has been before the public."

New York Telegram

"IT is all excitement, outdoors and action, with danger by bullet, knife, fire and rope hovering over every reel, and love splashed through the theme with a heavy brush."

New York Journal

A WILLIAM S. HART PRODUCTION

Adapted by Bennet Musson

Directed by Lambert Hillyer
Photographed by Joe August, A.S.C.

A Paramount Picture

The crowning achievement
of a brilliant career —

DOUGLAS FAIRBANKS

presents

"The Three
Musketeers"

BASED ON THAT IMMORTAL NOVEL
BY ALEXANDRE DUMAS

Adaption, Costuming,
Research under
EDWARD KNOBLOCK

Direction under
FRED NIBLO

Photography under
ARTHUR EDESON

UNITED ARTISTS
CORPORATION

MARY PICKFORD   CHARLIE CHAPLIN
DOUGLAS FAIRBANKS   D. W. GRIFFITH
HIRAM ABRAMS, PRESIDENT

Pinnacle Productions, Inc.
present
NEAL HART
IN
"DANGER VALLEY"

DISTRIBUTED BY
INDEPENDENT FILMS ASS'N

SPEED—ACTION
THRILLS—CHILLS
SUSPENSE—
AND A
CONTINUOUS
GALE OF
LAUGHTER!
REEL
FOR
REEL—
LAUGH
FOR
LAUGH—
"NOW OR
NEVER"
EXCELS
ANY
COMEDY
EVER
MADE—
HUMAN
WHOLESOME
HILARIOUS
CLEAN
CLEVER

COME AND
BRING YOUR
WIFE AND
CHILD
HAROLD
LLOYD
IS
RUNNING
WILD IN
HIS FIRST
MULTIPLE
REEL
SUPER
COMEDY

HAROLD LLOYD

IN HIS LARGEST, LONGEST AND LAUGHINGEST COMEDY.

NOW OR NEVER

HERE'S THE BIG EVENT!

Dick Barthelmess, now a star in his own right, heading his own company, makes his first picture.

And what a picture—an epic of mountain mothers and mountain men!

And a boy who leaps to manhood in life's greatest test!

ONE OF THE THREE BIGGEST DRAMAS OF THE YEAR—AND THAT'S THE PLAIN, UNVARNISHED TRUTH!

Richard Barthelmess in

Tol'able David

A FIRST
NATIONAL
ATTRACTION

GLADYS
HULETTE
IN IT, TOO!

33

William S. Hart in

"3 WORD BRAND"

A WILD WEST romance that makes Buffalo Bill's show as tame as a sewing circle.

With Hart in three roles — a pioneer, a plainsman, and the Governor of the State!

Starting with a lone man's fight with a tribe of savage Indians.

You'll see Hart rescue the girl from under the hoofs of a maddened steer. You'll see him kidnap the governor, take his place, and save his friend from hanging. You'll see him fight with guns and fists. You'll see the mightiest climax a picture ever had.

Hart's in the thick of all the action—and the action sure is thick!

A picture that would make even a college president stand up and cheer!

By Will Reynolds

Adapted and directed by Lambert Hillyer

Photographed by Joe August. A. S. C.

A William S. Hart Production

FAMOUS PLAYERS LASKY CORPORATION
ADOLPH ZUKOR and JESSE L. LASKY present CECIL B. DE MILLE Director General
NEW YORK

A Paramount Picture

1922

Gloria Swanson pulled out all stops for fancy headdresses in *Her Gilded Cage,* while Charlie Chaplin was putting cake icing on his hat in his four-reel comedy *The Pilgrim.* Valentino came through with one of his best pictures, *Blood and Sand,* and the not-so-successful *The Young Rajah.* Marion Davies and Douglas Fairbanks starred in two of the biggest costume pictures of the year, *When Knighthood Was in Flower* and *Robin Hood.* Tom Mix was king of the westerns and Harold Lloyd made his first five-reel comedy, *Grandma's Boy.*

A
Paramount
Picture

SIXTH of the "Famous 41," this will be a sensation everywhere. Can you imagine Glorious Gloria as the dancing sensation of Paris—with over a score of daring, dazzling dance costumes?

David Powell, Harrison Ford and Walter Hiers are in the cast.

A Sam Wood Production

FAMOUS PLAYERS·LASKY CORPORATION

From the play by
Ann Nichols
Scenario by
Elmer Harris and
Percy Heath.

JESSE L·LASKY
PRESENTS

GLORIA SWANSON
in "Her Gilded Cage"

37

NEW

Special Notice
Performances Start:
10 A. M., 12 Noon, 2.20,
4.40, 7.00 & 9.00 P. M

Prices:
Matinee: Orchestra, 44c
        Balcony. 25c
Nights: Orchestra........75c
        First Balcony..44c
        Second Balcony 25c

ANOTHER WEEK!
Thousands Still Want To See

Original Music Score
As Played In
New York City

DOUGLAS FAIRBANKS in "ROBIN HOOD"

DELIGHTFUL
ENID
BENNETT
In the Supporting Cast

Rich with romance—thick with thrills—

Stupendous scenes of regal splendor as a setting for the age-old story of Robin Hood and his merry bandits.

Douglas Fairbanks has gone beyond anything he has ever done before. He has made a picture which for magnificence of setting, richness of pageantry, beauty and elegance of photography and impressiveness of action has probably never been equaled before: surely not surpassed.—NEW YORK TIMES

It seems so colossal that one wonders how a star, a director or a screen writer could ever have had the courage to tackle it.—NEW YORK TRIBUNE.

It is the most ravishingly beautiful picture that has ever graced our screen. Every single scene is a delight to the eye, even while the stirring action grips the heart.
—NEW YORK DAILY NEWS.

No part that we can think of would fit an actor better than this title role falls about the athletic shoulders of Douglas Fairbanks. The cast is well-nigh perfect.
—NEW YORK EVENING WORLD.

ALL
NEXT
WEEK.

BIJOU

Matinees, 30c;
Evenings, 40c,
Tax Included.

Where Laughter Reigns—And Joy It Pours

HAROLD LLOYD

in

Grandma's Boy

His first *5* part feature

Each scene a scream
Each bit a hit
Each reel a riot

Surprise in
Climax.

LAUGHTER
all the way.

A howl at the
finish.

'Grandma's Boy' Is to Lloyd What 'The Kid' Was to Charley Chaplin
More Laughs, More Heart Pulls Than Any Comedy Ever Given the Screen

ADOLPH ZUKOR
PRESENTS

AGNES AYRES

in

'A Daughter Of Luxury'

A Paramount Picture

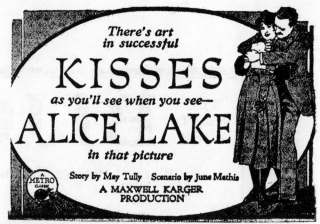

There's art
in successful

KISSES

as you'll see when you see—

ALICE LAKE

in that picture

Story by May Tully   Scenario by June Mathis

A MAXWELL KARGER
PRODUCTION

A METRO CLASSIC

RODOLPH VALENTINO

IN

"Blood and Sand"

WITH
LILA LEE AND NITA NALDI

THE whole world wants to see Valentino as the dashing toreador in this great tale of love and adventure.

"Blood and Sand" is the masterpiece of the author of "The Four Horsemen," and produced by Fred Niblo, who made "The Three Musketeers," it will be one of the two biggest pictures of the year.

A Paramount Picture

D. W. GRIFFITH

presents

'Orphans of
the Storm'

Adapted from

'The Two Orphans'

By arrangement with Kate Claxton
With Lillian and Dorothy Gish

Can a Woman Love More Than One Man?

Young, slim, wistful, and country-bred, she went to Paris with her blind sister. Kidnapped, she is saved by an aristocrat. She met Danton, the leader. The love of these two for Henriette Girard, her love for them, is the golden cord D. W. Griffith has interwoven through "Orphans of the Storm."

UNITED ARTISTS CORPORATION

Joseph M. Schenck presents

CONSTANCE TALMADGE

in

"EAST IS WEST"

8 Reels of the Best Ever

THIS is the great picture that Ellis Parker Butler, author of "Pigs is Pigs", wrote 6 advertisements about in THE SATURDAY EVENING POST.

Ellis Parker Butler

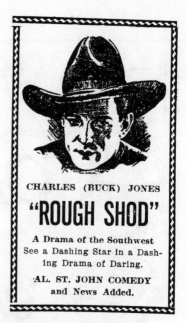

CHARLES (BUCK) JONES
"ROUGH SHOD"

A Drama of the Southwest
See a Dashing Star in a Dashing Drama of Daring.

AL. ST. JOHN COMEDY
and News Added.

PARKWAY

MAGNIFICENT

*Critics Have Acclaimed It With
Torrents Of Praise*

MARION DAVIES

IN

"WHEN KNIGHTHOOD WAS IN FLOWER"

From the Novel by Charles Major

In the Supporting Cast
Forrest Stanley and Lyn Harding

The thrills of a lifetime—the rich romance of a hundred love masterpieces.

PARKWAY CONCERT ORCHESTRA
V. NESSUL, DIRECTOR
NEXT WEEK
"KENTUCKY DERBY"
The Great Race Drama

42

JESSE L. LASKY PRESENTS

Rodolph Valentino

IN

"THE YOUNG RAJAH"

CAST INCLUDES

WANDA HAWLEY

— AND —

CHARLES OGLE

Another World-Beater!

YOU'LL find "The Young Rajah" a worthy successor to "Blood and Sand."

Valentino the magnificent in another exotic, fascinating role, in a story the like of which has never been screened.

Costumes and sets of unparalleled beauty, and a climax so thrilling you'll never forget it.

From the play "Amos Judd"
by Alethea Luce and the novel
by John Ames Mitchell.
Scenario by June Mathis.
Directed by Philip E. Rosen.

A Paramount Picture

FAMOUS PLAYERS-LASKY CORPORATION

43

THIS big stage hit makes a sure-fire picture. One of the greatest casts ever assembled, and a production in which no expense has been spared.

It will be one of the most talked-of pictures of the year.

From the play by Rachel Crothers. Screen play by Clara Beranger.

A *Paramount Picture*

ADOLPH ZUKOR PRESENTS A

William de Mille
PRODUCTION
"NICE PEOPLE"
WITH
WALLACE REID
BEBE DANIELS
CONRAD NAGEL
JULIA FAYE

FAMOUS PLAYERS-LASKY CORPORATION
— ADOLPH ZUKOR, President —
NEW YORK CITY

44

Created by Cosmopolitan Productions

FAMOUS PLAYERS—LASKY CORP
PRESENTS

"THE VALLEY OF SILENT MEN"

WITH **Alma Rubens**
A Paramount Picture

From the Famous Story of
JAS. OLIVER CURWOOD

Bigger and Better Than "River's
End!" A Gripping Drama of
Great Souls, and Strong,
Waging Their Battles of
Love and Life in the
Frozen North

ACTUALLY FILMED MIDST
THE CANADIAN ROCKIES

BLUEBIRD

LAST SHOWING TODAY

William Fox
presents

SHIRLEY MASON
in
YOUTH MUST HAVE LOVE

*A Pulsating Drama
of Romance and
Mystery*

Cast Includes
WALLACE McDONALD
Special Added
"STEP LIVELY, PLEASE"
A New Sunshine Comedy and
International News

Starting Saturday

A Two-Star Bull's-Eye!

Thundering hoofs and
alkali, a beautiful girl
and a fighting man—
a sweeping drama of
the Great Southwest!

JACK HOLT
AND
BEBE DANIELS
IN
"North of the Rio Grande"

A Paramount Picture

Last
Times
Friday—
Constance
Talmadge
in
"The
Primitive
Lover!"

Liberty

DIRECTION of JENSEN-VON HERBERG
MALOTTE AT THE WURLITZER

Also a
Mack
Sennett
Comedy!
Ben
Turpin in
"Step
Forward!"

ALWAYS THE BEST FOR THE LIBERTY GUEST

Metropolitan

NORTH AVE. AT PENNSYLVANIA

Performances: 1.30, 3.30, 5.30, 7.30, 9.30 P. M.

MARY PICKFORD

Come to the matinee if possible.

IN
Exclusive First Showing

OF

A BRAND NEW TEN REEL PICTURIZATION

OF

GRACE MILLER WHITE'S GREATEST STORY

"Tess of the Storm Country"

The Beautiful Mary Pickford

As a girl again—More beautiful than ever—with the sunny curls and tawdry tatters, roguish smile, quaint impudence, of the inimitable Tess. An entirely new picture—as new as it is beautiful—so gripping that it hurts—so superb that it awes. The crowning achievement of Mary Pickford's career.

Not an old scene in the whole film

Next Attraction—ALICE BRADY IN "THE LEOPARDESS"
By Katharine Newlin Burt. Now Ruuning In The Morning Sun

WILLIAM S.
HART
IN
"Travelin' On"
A Paramount Picture

SEE him fight the worst town in the West!—fight through the wildest storm scenes ever filmed!—fight for a great love!—fight for his better self and win!

IMPERIAL

ENTIRE WEEK
The lad who makes the world laugh!

HAROLD
LLOYD
IN
Dr. Jack
Five Reels of Laughter

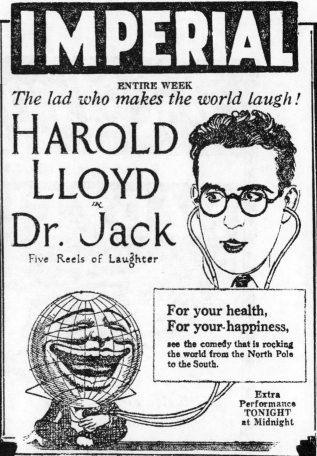

For your health,
For your happiness,
see the comedy that is rocking the world from the North Pole to the South.

Extra
Performance
TONIGHT
at Midnight

THESE——
did not
conquer him

but—
THIS
!

A MAN'S thrilling battle for his own soul in the romantic South Seas!

Jack Holt IN
"The Man Unconquerable"
Beautiful SYLVIA BREAMER is back in this Paramount Picture

SHIRLEY
MASON
IN
The NEW TEACHER

You know the infallible charm of this daintiest of screen stars. See her in this, her latest, production. She'll win your heart once more.

AL ST. JOHN COMEDY
AND NEWS ADDED

Does Cave-manning
pay?

Is it true of girls that

They Like 'Em Rough

Viola Dana

in this picture shows whether
they do or not

A METRO CLASSIC

BLUEBIRD

Today and Through Thursday

A MYSTERY
ROMANCE OF
THE RANGE

DIRECTED BY
LYNN REYNOLDS

William Fox
presents

Tom Mix

in

For Big Stakes

See the Greatest Picture Ever
Enacted by Tom Mix
Extra Added
Last Time Today
"The Adventures of Sherlock
Holmes"
"A Case of Identity"
Also News Wed. and Thurs.
Sunshine Comedy Added.

TODAY
TOMOR.
& SAT.
(3 DAYS)

—COLONIAL—

Daily at 11,
12:45, 2:30,
4:15, 6, 7:45
and 9:30

Come and See Wallie Beat Up an Army of Ghosts!

SEE him clean out a
haunted castle—and
win the beautiful Spanish
Princess! It's a gay tale
of adventure and love.
Thousands laughed at the
stage play—millions will
scream with delight at the
picture.

**With the Best Comedy
Cast in History**

JESSE L. LASKY
PRESENTS

WALLACE REID

in

"The Ghost Breaker"

SUPPORTED BY

LILA LEE and WALTER HIERS

a Paramount Picture

Also a ROLIN COMEDY

1923

The era of silent movies was one in which people heard a lot of good music. One of the pleasant things to remember was the organ music you heard upon entering the theater. Most of the large theaters employed a concert orchestra, but when the orchestra wasn't in the pit, their place was not taken by ragtime-playing pianists. Organists took over. And in theaters that had no orchestras, organists had the entire job of playing music cued to the screen dramas. That was how it was in 1923 when Jackie Coogan, the most famous child actor in the world was seen in *Oliver Twist,* and Harold Lloyd was hanging from the hands of a clock in *Safety Last.*

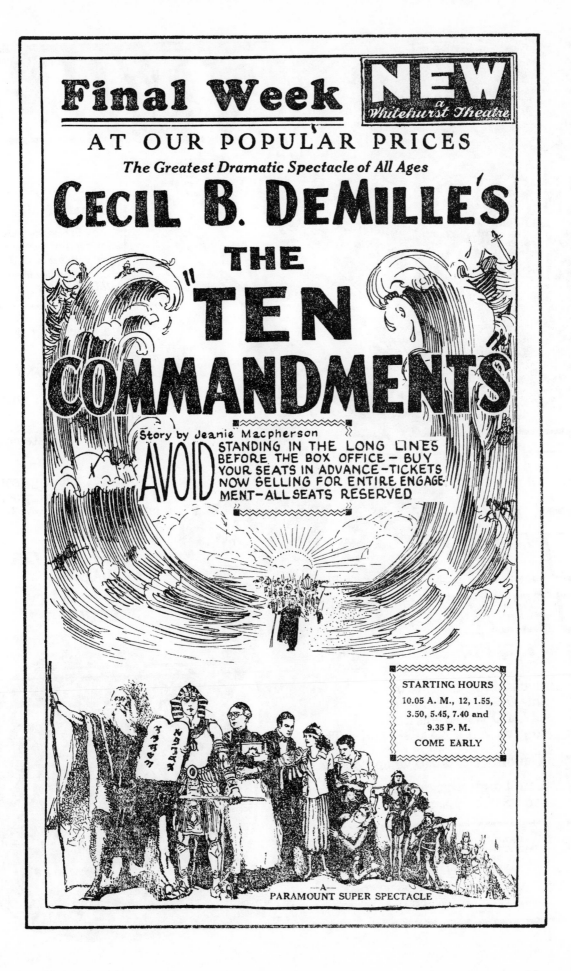

Laughter First!

RIVOLI

Harold Lloyd

Please Note:
For this engagement only our first performance will begin at 11 A. M., then continuous to 11.30 P. M.

Twelve stories up and only one way to fall.

And that's DOWN!

You'll explode with laughter!

You'll have Hysterics of joy!

You'll get the biggest thrill and biggest laugh you ever had in your life.

LAUGH AND LET LAUGH!

TRY "SAFETY LAUGHS"

In climbing the side of this 12-story building LLOYD risked his life to give you a LAUGH and a Thrill.

You only risk a rib when you see it.

You laugh with safety when you see "Safety Last."

ADDED ATTRACTIONS
MANILLA POWERS, LYRIC SOPRANO
"WEEPING WATERS," AN INDIAN LEGEND
OF THE OREGON COUNTRY
AESOP'S FABLES—RIVOLI NEWS

RIVOLI SYMPHONY ORCHESTRA
FELICE IULA, CONDUCTING

IN HIS FIRST SEVEN REEL COMEDY

Safety Last

A THRILL-A-MINUTE A LAUGH-A-SECOND

A COMEDY CYCLONE

VIOLA DANA

IN

HER FATAL MILLIONS

A METRO PICTURE

A Society Snob—

'till pa-pa's young assistant came along. He taught her a thing or two about the game of love.

It has heart interest, pathos, comedy.

The COSMOPOLITAN CORPORATION presents

"The Love Piker"

WITH

ANITA STEWART

Directed by
E. MASON HOPPER
By FRANK R. ADAMS
A Cosmopolitan Production

Thursday and Friday

WILLIAM S. HART
"Wild Bill Hickok"

NEW THEATRE

Continuous 10 A. M. to 11 P. M.

New Theatre Concert Orchestra
Charles Weisman, Conducting

HIS FIRST METRO PICTURE

America's Film Idol

JACKIE COOGAN

in

LONG LIVE THE KING"

By Mary Roberts Rinehart

A romance of golden youth, royal love and thrilling adventure, in which Jackie appears as the boy prince of everybody's dreams amid the sensational intrigue of a Balkan court

A Critic Says

He displays in this picture that he is fully worthy of the production. It is the first "big" film ever made with a child star. Jackie shoulders the responsibility beautifully and as the Crown Prince Otto of Livonia, he gives the most distinguished performance of his short career. — N. Y. Telegraph.

A METRO PICTURE

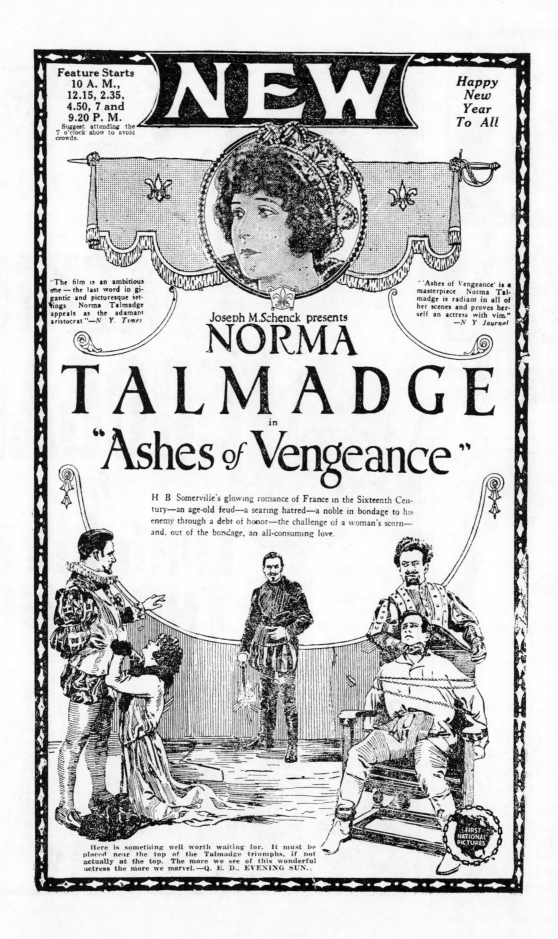

54

NEW

A Goldwyn Cosmopolitan Production

Cosmopolitan Corporation presents

MARION DAVIES IN "LITTLE OLD NEW YORK"

Harrison Ford

Adapted by Luther Reed from the stage play by Rida Johnson Young With A Wonderful Cast Including

Harrison Ford
Mahlon Hamilton
Montague Love
and Louis Wolheim

Montague Love

Irresistible charm and thrilling action make this story of the days when America was young a truly great picture entertainment.

The New York Critics Say:

And if we know anything about cinema acting and cinema directing and designing, here is one of the loveliest and simplest love stories which have come to the screen in a season, performed almost perfectly from start to finish.—New York World.

For costumes and settings and photography, "Little Old New York" is one of the most exquisite productions ever thrown on a screen.—New York Times.

Played Cosmopolitan Theatre 8 weeks at $2 top. Now in second capacity week at Capitol, the largest Film Theatre in the world.

Feature Starts
10 A. M., 12.15, 2.35, 4.50, 7 and 9.20 P. M.

Suggest attending the 7 o'clock show to avoid crowds

NEW THEATRE

The Season's Breeziest Romance!

Continuous 10 A. M. to 11 P. M.

FASTER! FASTER!

That's the tingling cry when youth's at the wheel— when a girl's love and a man's honor depend on taking whirl-wind chances. You'll be gripped by the breathless thrill of it; you'll laugh as you zip along

NEW THEATRE CONCERT ORCHESTRA

ADOLPH ZUKOR PRESENTS

AGNES AYRES

In the Paramount Picture

"Racing Hearts"

THEODORE ROBERTS and RICHARD DIX IN THE SUPPORTING CAST

METROPOLITAN

NORTH AVE. AT PENNSYLVANIA
Beginning Easter Monday
At 11 A.M. Continuous Till 11 P. M.

5 MONTHS ON BROADWAY AT $2 PRICES **3** WEEKS IN BALTIMORE AT $1.65 PRICES

HERE AT OUR REGULAR PRICES

Nothing Can Compare With This Great Romance of a Love That Outlived Passion

LILLIAN GISH
IN
"The WHITE SISTER"
From F. MARION CRAWFORD'S novel

LILLIAN GISH

DRAMA

Lillian Gish as the girl tricked out of her fortune, her own lover sought by her scheming half-sister.

THRILLS

A fight on the desert (filmed in Algeria.) A cross-country hunt, filmed in the old-world beauty of Italy.

57

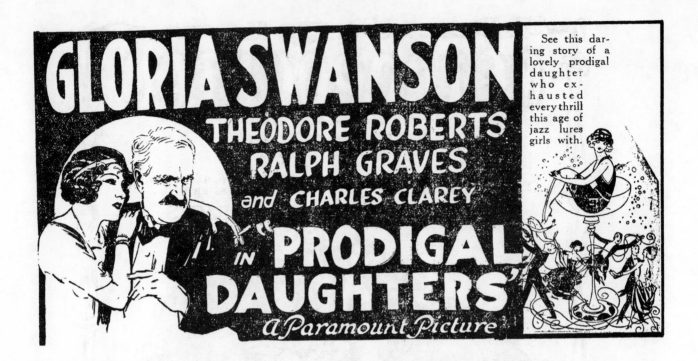

Boulevard

33rd St. and Greenmount Ave.
Air Changed Every 5 Minutes
*Music by Original Boulevard Orchestra
Under the Direction of Mr. Sokolove.*

Monday and Tuesday Only
Special Added Attraction
2,000 Feet of Pictures, Showing the
Japanese Earthquake

Monday, Tuesday, Wednesday

ADOLPH ZUKOR PRESENTS
"LAWFUL LARCENY"
WITH
HOPE HAMPTON
NITA NALDI
LEW CODY
CONRAD NAGEL
—An Allan Dwan Production—

Thursday and Friday
WILLIAM S.
HART.
'SINGER
JIM McKEE'
A William S Hart Production
A Paramount Picture

WILLIAM FOX *presents*
Tom Mix
IN
MILE-A-
MINUTE ROMEO

CONTINUOUS 10 A. M. TO 11 P. M.
FEATURE STARTS
10 A. M., 1.45, 3.45, 5.50, 7.55
and 9.50 P. M.

NEW

It's here at Last!

GET READY FOR LAUGHS

JOSEPH M. SCHENCK
presents

BUSTER KEATON

IN

"Three Ages"

HIS FIRST
6 REEL
COMEDY
FEATURE

Metro Picture

**EXTRA ADDED
ATTRACTION**

REGINALD DENNY

—IN—

"The Wandering Two"

By H. C. WITWER
Author of Original Leather
Pushers

**Read What a
Critic Says About It**

Keaton has never been
more seriously funny. There
isn't an incident in all the
six reels that does not keep
the audience in genuine
good humor.—SAN FRAN-
CISCO EXAMINER.

59

DUSTIN FARNUM
IN
The Man Who Won

Directed by William Wellman

New Glory
for Gloria

CENTURY

ADOLPH ZUKOR
PRESENTS

GLORIA SWANSON

IN

"ZAZA"

AN ALLAN DWAN
PRODUCTION

A
Paramount Picture

GLORIA SWANSON as "Zaza!" And such a "Zaza!" A living volcano of furious loves, hates and jealousies, illuminating this famous old love drama with the light of new-born greatness.

Produced by the maker of "Robin Hood," "Lawful Larceny," etc.

From the Play by Pierre
Berton and Charles Simon

61

HAL ROACH PRESENTS

Harold Lloyd

in

"Why Worry?"

HIS LATEST SIX REEL

Pathécomedy
TRADE MARK

Heart-ache!
Head-ache! or
Tooth-ache!

Forget 'em all.
You'll have an ear-to-
ear-ache from
laughter.

See "Why Worry?"
then you'll say
"Why Worry?"

The bigger they are
The heartier they laugh.

1924

John Barrymore returned from Broadway to star for Warner Brothers in *Beau Brummel,* while John Gilbert was just beginning his years at Metro-Goldwyn-Mayer, appearing with Lon Chaney in *He Who Gets Slapped.* Lillian Gish went to Italy to make *Romola,* while Richard Barthelmess was at West Point to film *Classmates.* One of the biggest pictures of the year was *The Sea Hawk* with Milton Sills, and Rin Tin Tin was the most famous dog star on the screen. Hoot Gibson and Jack Hoxie were starring in fast action westerns at Universal and packing the small town theaters on Saturday afternoons.

Thursday, Friday, Saturday
"CODE OF THE SEA"
with
Rod La Rocque, Jacqueline Logan
VICTOR FLEMING
A Paramount Picture

IMPERIAL

Today

"The Fighting SAP"

with

FRED THOMSON

and his

Marvelous Horse
SILVER KING

If you like cyclonic action, if powerful drama appeals to you, if you respond to exquisite romance, if you're entertained by a real Western photodrama full of every element that has made movies popular, by all means SEE THIS PICTURE!

—Other Features—

Comedy   Fox
Dancing Daisies'   News

Imperial Concert Orchestra

MADISON

Starting Tomorrow for Four Days

THE BIG COMPANION PICTURE TO "THE COVERED WAGON"
Another Super-Thrilling Western Pioneer Romance

By the Same Author

EMERSON HOUGH

NEVER SUCH THRILLS!

—the wild stampede of thousands of frenzied long-horn cattle.
—the Indians attacking the cowboy escort
A thrilling spectacle, a stirring romance, a living record of early American history.

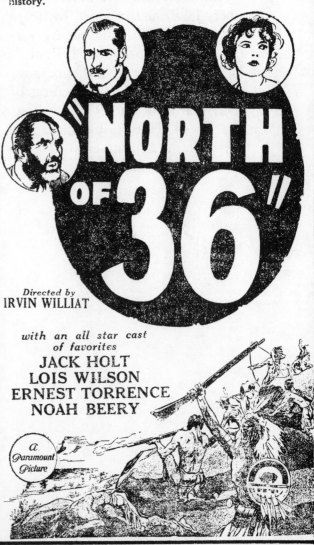

"NORTH OF 36"

Directed by
IRVIN WILLIAT

with an all star cast of favorites
JACK HOLT
LOIS WILSON
ERNEST TORRENCE
NOAH BEERY

A Paramount Picture

NEW THEATRE

TODAY 12:45

DOORS
OPEN
SUNDAYS
ONLY
AT 12:30

*The Most
Beautiful
Picture of
theSeason!*

JACKIE COOGAN
in
A BOY OF FLANDERS

Sunshine and shadows—joy and sorrow—love and ambition—each in turn play their consummate parts in the life of Nello, the orphan, and his four-footed pal, Petrasche.

"A BOY OF FLANDERS" is an adaptation of Ouida's immortal classic, "A Dog of Flanders," read and loved by millions.

A Great Cast Including
**Josef Swickard, Nigel de Brulier
Lionel Belmore and Nell Craig**

A Metro Picture

ONLY ONE WEEK

RIVOLI

Continuous—
12 Noon
To 11.30 P. M.

*In Commemoration of the City Securing
the Army and Navy Game—*

*We Take Pleasure in Presenting as Our
Thanksgiving Week Attraction—*

Richard Barthelmess
in
Classmates

From the Play by William C. De Mille
and Margaret Turnbull

The Idol of a Nation—
The dream of every boy—
The hope of every girl—
Our Dick was never great-
er than as the heroic cadet
of West Point who was a
real man even in the face
of the greatest odds.

Made at West Point
with the full co-opera-
tion of the United
States Military.

FIRST NATIONAL PICTURES

Added Attractions
Mack Sennett
Presents
Harry Langdon
in
*"The Hansom
Cabman"*
Rivoli Presentation
Return of the Favorite
HARRY BREUER
Xylophone Marvel

A First National Picture

RIVOLI SYMPHONY ORCHESTRA, FELICE IULA CONDUCTING

66

Constance Talmadge in *Her Night of Romance*

Bebe Daniels in "Dangerous Money"

"THE FAST SET"
a WILLIAM deMILLE *Production*
PRESENTED BY ADOLPH ZUKOR *and* JESSE L. LASKY
BETTY COMPSON
ADOLPHE MENJOU
ELLIOTT DEXTER
ZASU PITTS
a Paramount Picture

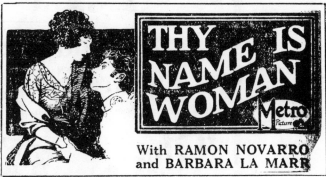

THY NAME IS WOMAN
Metro Picture
WITH RAMON NOVARRO
and BARBARA LA MARR

ONE OF *Paramount's* FAMOUS 40

A SIDNEY OLCOTT *Production*

ADOLPH ZUKOR
JESSE L. LASKY
PRESENT

RUDOLPH VALENTINO IN "Monsieur Beaucaire"

a Paramount Picture

with
BEBE DANIELS
LOIS WILSON
DORIS KENYON
LOWELL SHERMAN

From the novel by Booth Tarkington
and the play by Booth Tarkington
and Evelyn Greenleaf Sutherland
Screen play by Forrest Halsey

A RARE TREAT

RIVOLI

CONTINUOUS
12 NOON
TO 11.30 P. M.

Second and Last Week of the Picture Sensation of 1924

The Greatest Spectacle of Amazing Romance and Adventure the World Has Ever Seen!

"The SEA HAWK"

By, Rafael Sabatini
Author of "Scaramouche"

—WITH—

MILTON SILLS

ENID BENNETT
MARC MacDERMOTT
LLOYD HUGHES
WALLACE BEERY
And a Cast of Thousands

This
Is
Movie
Week

A First National Picture

FEATURE STARTS
12.15, 2.40, 5.00, 7.25, 9.45

NOTICE!
Admission Prices for
"The Sea Hawk"
Matinee:
Balcony, 30c   Orchestra, 50c
Evenings:
Balcony, 40c   Orchestra, 66c

Ask those who have seen "The Sea Hawk"—then if you miss it, you will owe yourself an apology.

RIVOLI SYMPHONY ORCHESTRA, FELICE IULA CONDUCTING

68

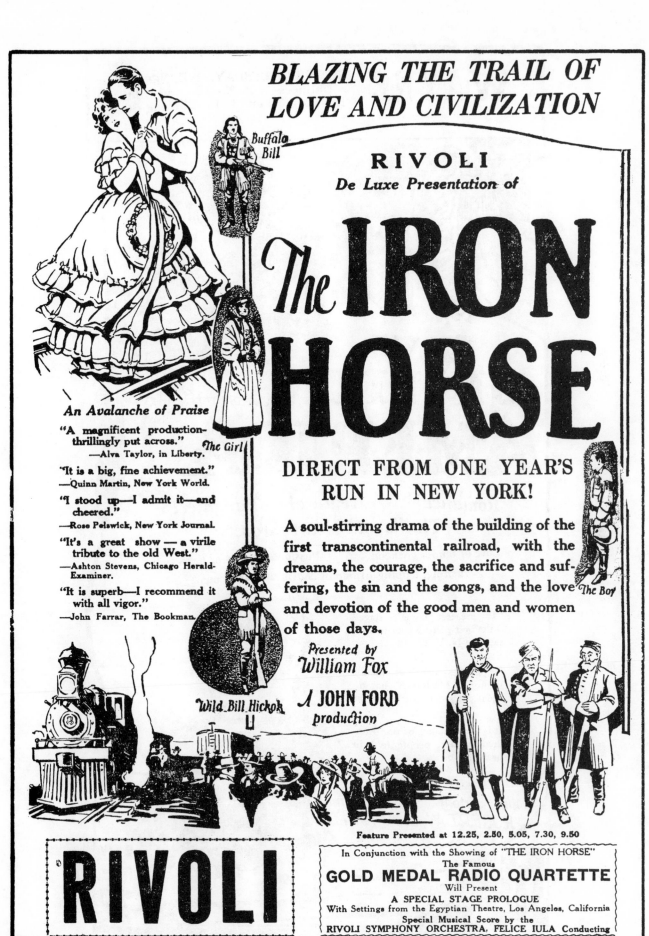

BLAZING THE TRAIL OF LOVE AND CIVILIZATION

Buffalo Bill

RIVOLI
De Luxe Presentation of

The IRON HORSE

The Girl

DIRECT FROM ONE YEAR'S RUN IN NEW YORK!

A soul-stirring drama of the building of the first transcontinental railroad, with the dreams, the courage, the sacrifice and suffering, the sin and the songs, and the love and devotion of the good men and women of those days.

The Boy

Presented by
William Fox

A JOHN FORD production

Wild Bill Hickok

An Avalanche of Praise

"A magnificent production—thrillingly put across."
—Alva Taylor, in Liberty.

"It is a big, fine achievement."
—Quinn Martin, New York World.

"I stood up—I admit it—and cheered."
—Rose Pelswick, New York Journal.

"It's a great show — a virile tribute to the old West."
—Ashton Stevens, Chicago Herald-Examiner.

"It is superb—I recommend it with all vigor."
—John Farrar, The Bookman.

Feature Presented at 12.25, 2.50, 5.05, 7.30, 9.50

RIVOLI

In Conjunction with the Showing of "THE IRON HORSE"
The Famous
GOLD MEDAL RADIO QUARTETTE
Will Present
A SPECIAL STAGE PROLOGUE
With Settings from the Egyptian Theatre, Los Angeles, California
Special Musical Score by the
RIVOLI SYMPHONY ORCHESTRA, FELICE IULA Conducting

WAYNE

TONIGHT, TUESDAY, WEDNESDAY
Matinees--2 P. M.--20c and 35c
Nights--6:30 and 8:45--25c and 50c

Just recently shown at the Victory, Dayton, at $1.65 top.

D·W· GRIFFITH presents
AMERICA

Romance!   Adventure!   Laughter!
Thrills and Heart-throbs!

Love of tender girlhood   Passionate deeds of heroes
A rushing, leaping drama of charm and excitement

"The greatest play ever staged ---the best picture ever made." says the *N. Y. World*

"It pulsates with life; and for beauty, 'AMERICA' has no equal", says *Theatre Magazine*

It is the romance of one hundred million people told in heart-throbs

a thrilling story of Love and Romance
ROBERT W. CHAMBERS

WESLEY BARRY
IN
"The PRINTER'S DEVIL"

With HARRY MYERS
And a Notable Cast

A rollicking romance of a small-town newspaper,
with the freckled-face boy as the very devil of a
printer's devil.

*A Warner Bros.
Classic*

Pola Negri
In "Men"

The full fire of her genius
burns vividly in this merci-
less expose of the way
rich men make love.

CECIL B.
DeMILLE'S
"TRIUMPH"
WITH
LEATRICE JOY, ROD La ROCQUE

THE creator of "The Ten Commandments"
breaks his own record for lavishness with
"Triumph." The whirl of fashionable society
and the world of modern industry moulded
into the most luscious screen feast since De
Mille's "Male and Female" and "Man-
slaughter."

THE FILM SENSATION!

SELDOM does the screen echo the heart-
beat of humanity as does this great motion picture. The tears, the laughter, the joy
of life are the fabrics of which *Victor Sea-
strom* has woven a truly immortal masterpiece.

WITH
LON CHANEY
NORMA SHEARER
JOHN GILBERT
TULLY MARSHALL
FORD STERLING
CLYDE COOK

VICTOR SEASTROM'S PRODUCTION

He
Who gets
Slapped

*from the great
Stage Success by*
LEONID ANDREYEV
Adapted by CAREY WILSON
Produced by
LOUIS B. MAYER

A
Metro
Goldwyn
Picture

NATIONAL

Today—Tomorrow—Wednesday

Hours of
Showing
1, 3, 5, 7, 9

HAVE YOU EVER seen a Magic Rug soar above the city bearing a Thief and a Princess?

Have you ever seen a white horse with wings fly thru the clouds?

Douglas Fairbanks
in
"The THIEF of BAGDAD"

Have you ever seen Magic ropes, live dragons and bats as big as elephants?

Have you ever seen an "invisible" cloak?

This beautiful story of romance and adventure abounds in happenings of astounding and unbelievable magic.

The Original Musical Score. National Wonder Orchestra, Vincent Kay, conducting.

Corinne Griffith in Love's Wilderness

A First National Picture

THOMAS MEIGHAN

Presented by
ADOLPH ZUKOR
JESSE L. LASKY

A Paramount Picture

in "THE ALASKAN"

by
JAMES OLIVER CURWOOD

A HERBERT BRENON PRODUCTION

Adolph Zukor
Jesse L. Lasky
present

GLORIA SWANSON in
"A Society Scandal"

An
Allan Dwan
Production

A Paramount Picture

Gloria in silks and laces, Gloria in furbelows, Gloria wearing gowns as only she can wear them. But a vital, flashing, dramatic Gloria in a dramatic love-comedy, full of entertainment, full of charm, full of thrill.

NORMA TALMADGE *in* *The Only Woman*

ADOLPH ZUKOR AND JESSE L. LASKY PRESENT
RICHARD DIX *in* **"Manhattan"**
a Paramount Picture

C. C. BURR presents

Johnny Hines
IN "*The* **SPEED SPOOK**"

*The Snappiest, Speediest Dramatic Comedy
Ever Filmed*

A Whirlwind of Recklessness, Romance and
Sparkling Humor

WEEK BEGINNING MONDAY, MARCH 24—MATINEES DAILY

World's Premier Presentation of the Most Beautiful Romance
in all History

AMERICA'S MOST DISTINGUISHED ACTOR

JOHN BARRYMORE
in "BEAU BRUMMEL"

SPECIALLY ARRANGED SYMPHONY ORCHESTRA OF
25 PIECES

Daily Matinees, 50c to $1.00.   Nights, 50c to $1.50.   SEATS NOW—LYCEUM AND ALBAUGH'S.

G·A·R·D·E·N
Cor. Garden-Adams

TODAY—SUNDAY ONLY

A SPARKLING, BUBBLING DRAUGHT
—IT FIZZES AND FOAMS WITH
GLEE - -

Johnny Hines
EARLY BIRD

THRILLS—ADVENTURE—FUN

*A ragged kid from 'Frisco suddenly finds
himself cast up on a desert island, a black
cat his only companion—until—cannibals—
attacks—the marines—the San Francisco
police force—adventure—romance—thrills
—and laughs with—*

JackieCoogan
in
Little Robinson Crusoe

By
WILLARD MACK

Supervised by
JACK COOGAN, Sr.

FEATURE TIME—
10.33 A. M., 12.10,
2.10, 4.17, 5.58,
8.07, 10.10 P. M.

*Colorful with splashes of
sunlight and gorgeous
with exotic birds and
foliage. Picturesque,
thrilling and with
comedy laughing
through the tears of
a great story.*

74

POSITIVELY ONE WEEK ONLY

A Lifetime of Laughter Crowded Into Seven Rousing Reels

Harold Lloyd

in Girl Shy

The Prince of Merry-Makers

At His Best—
In His Best—

Ain't it a G-r-r-rand
and Glorious Feelin'?

*Here he is! The lad whose
waggery makes the whole
world kin!*

*And Boy, Oh, Boy, what
a comedy!*

A Merry Whirl of Laughter
Love and Thrills!

A Pathé Picture

75

1925

By now there were nearly 15,000 movie theaters in operation in the United States and it was a very good year for them. Some of the biggest money-makers of the decade were released. Among them such famous films as *Don Q, Son of Zorro, The Phantom of the Opera, The Freshman,* and, after two years in production, Charlie Chaplin's *The Gold Rush.* Richard Dix was elevated to stardom at Paramount and Tom Mix starred in two of his best pictures, *The Deadwood Coach* and *The Rainbow Trail,* while Gary Cooper was just starting in pictures playing bit parts in westerns.

WILLIAM FOX
presents

TOM MIX
in ZANE GREY'S

"THE RAINBOW TRAIL"

The Sequel to
Riders of the
Purple Sage

WITH TONY, the Wonder Horse

He dreamt of the end of the trail and its reward

It Is Curwood's
Greatest Story
of the Great
Outdoors

JAMES OLIVER
CURWOOD'S
"THE ANCIENT
HIGHWAY"

AN IRVIN WILLAT PRODUCTION

WITH JACK HOLT
BILLIE DOVE
MONTAGU LOVE

PRESENTED BY
ADOLPH ZUKOR and JESSE L LASKY

Richard
Barthelmess
with
Dorothy Gish

in
The
BEAUTIFUL
CITY

First
National
Pictures

These two great stars were never
more wonderful!

COMEDY and RADIO DETECTIVE

"As Man Desires"

From
Gene Wright's Novel
"PANDORA LA CROIX"

with

MILTON
SILLS

and

VIOLA
DANA

Come to the place no
law can reach and live
through this drama of a
man who was robbed of
the greatest love and a
South Sea wildflower who
found it for him.

"I Love You
Strong
Man"

Pandora, the
South Sea beauty,
snuggled up to
this giant of a
man—

For a moment
her heart throbbed
to the beat of
his—

For a moment
he thought back
to another love—

FOR A MOMENT—

A First National Picture

FIRST
NATIONAL
PICTURES

POSITIVELY ONE WEEK ONLY!

With a whip for a weapon Douglas Fairbanks gives more laughs, more real thrills, more high speed, in "Don Q" than in any picture he has ever made.

DOUGLAS FAIRBANKS
"DON Q" SON OF ZORRO"
UNITED ARTISTS PICTURE.

The Finest Adventure Tale Ever Screened

The dashing, daring Don Q bars all worry and you live in laughs and thrills.

The Greatest Picture Fairbanks Has Ever Offered

Feature Presented at 12.25, 2.50, 5.05, 7.30, 9.50
De Luxe Shows at 2.30, 7.10, 9.30

80

TONIGHT
FOR 3 DAYS

Matinee Daily 2:15   Matinee 10c, 20c

Evening 7:00—9:00   Evening 10c, 20c, 30c

GORDON'S
STRAND

Here it is! The glamorous, glittering, glorious Graustark with our Norma living it in dramatic portrayal that puts her leaps and bounds ahead of all the rest. Thrills, intrigue, stolen moments — and amid it all one beautiful girl and a man fighting for love.

Big!   **Bigger!**   **Her Biggest**

with

Eugene O'Brien

George Barr McCutcheon

Screen Version Frances Marion

A Dimitri Buchowetski Production

First National Pictures

A First National Picture

NORMA *Talmadge* in **Graustark**

A Modern Romance in a Setting of Gold and Glory

HARRY CAREY
IN THE "TEXAS TRAIL"

AN intense, pulsating story of western daring and western bravery out in the great wide west where the language of the fist is the language of the land and where the court of justice is physical prowess and the might of the strongest.

And
TWO
BIG
Comedy
Riots

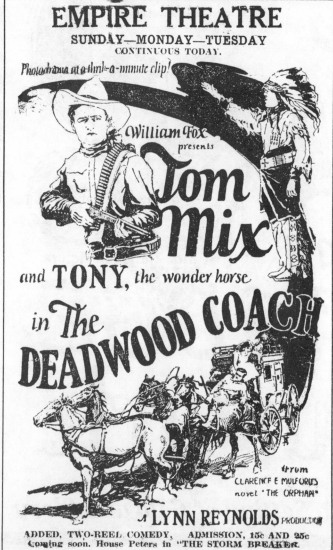

EMPIRE THEATRE
SUNDAY—MONDAY—TUESDAY
CONTINUOUS TODAY.

Photodrama at a thrill-a-minute clip!

William Fox presents

Tom Mix

and TONY, the wonder horse

in The

DEADWOOD COACH

from CLARENCE E MULFORD'S novel "THE ORPHAN"

A LYNN REYNOLDS PRODUCTION

ADDED, TWO-REEL COMEDY. ADMISSION, 15c AND 25c
Coming soon. House Peters in "THE STORM BREAKER"

ADOLPH ZUKOR and JESSE L. LASKY present

"THE LITTLE FRENCH GIRL"

a HERBERT BRENON PRODUCTION

WITH
ALICE JOYCE
NEIL HAMILTON
MARY BRIAN
ESTHER RALSTON

THE BEST SELLING BOOK IN AMERICA IS NOW A GREAT Paramount Picture

82

RICHARD DIX

a Paramount Picture

in

"WOMAN-HANDLED"

THE answer to "Manhandled" by the same author, Arthur Stringer.

GLORIA SWANSON said in "Manhandled," "Men won't let us alone!" Now Richard Dix says in "Womanhandled," "Women won't let us let them alone!"

POOR Richard! When they smiled, he fell!

MADISON

STARTING TODAY

DOUGLAS MacLEAN

a Paramount Picture

in

"7 Keys to Baldpate"

The World's Sweetheart

MARY PICKFORD

IN

"LITTLE ANNIE ROONEY"

From an Original Story by
Katherine Hennessey
Directed by William Beaudine

Mary in the ragamuffin and hoydenish type of role that made her beloved by millions. Her curls of gold again fly free, her mischievous smile and her prankish ways will fascinate and charm you.

Not Since "Daddy Longlegs" Has Mary Pickford Made a Picture More Appealing

Released by United Artists' Corporation

83

GRAND
HIGHLANDTOWN

Monday, Tuesday, Wednesday

RUGGED WATER
AN IRVIN WILLAT PRODUCTION
LOIS WILSON · WALLACE BEERY
WARNER BAXTER · PHYLLIS HAVER
A Paramount Picture

Thursday and Friday
Lewis Stone in

THE LADY who LIED

Sat.—CHARLIE CHAPLIN and
JACKIE COOGAN in "THE KID."

BOULEVARD
33D ST. AND GREENMOUNT AVE.
Music by Boulevard Orchestra Under Direction of Albert Sokolove.
MONDAY, TUESDAY, WEDNESDAY

NORMA SHEARER in her greatest role
Slave of Fashion with LEW CODY

Great
Metro Goldwyn Mayer

A Great Star in
Her Greatest Film!

THURSDAY, FRIDAY, SATURDAY
The HALF WAY Girl
With Doris Kenyon
A First National Picture

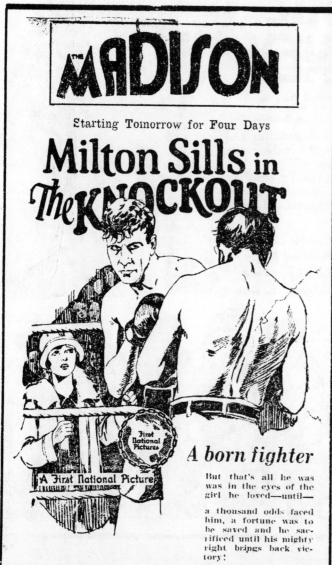

THE **MADISON**

Starting Tomorrow for Four Days

Milton Sills in
The KNOCKOUT

First National Pictures

A First National Picture

A born fighter

But that's all he was
was in the eyes of the
girl he loved—until—

a thousand odds faced
him, a fortune was to
be saved and he sac-
rificed until his mighty
right brings back vic-
tory!

APOLLO
Shows 11-1-3-5-7-9

A Great Modern
Comedy

MARION
DAVIES
in ZANDER
the GREAT
SUPPORTED BY
Harrison Ford
Hobart Bosworth
Harry Myers
Hedda Hopper
AND OTHER BIG STARS
ALSO
PATHE NEWS
ADV. OF MAZIE COMEDY

Adapted from the hilarious stage farce that
started its run thirty-three years ago. This
is unquestionably the funniest comedy ever

**Enough to make
a cat laugh**

"Charley's Aunt"

with

Syd Chaplin

IMPERIAL

Now at 11, 1, 3, 5, 7, 9
Feature 35 Minutes Later.

*Bebe
Daniels*
in
"MISS
BLUEBEARD"

PRESENTED BY
ADOLPH ZUKOR
JESSE L. LASKY

A Paramount Picture

A brilliant comedy drama of a
French beauty who found herself
with two husbands!

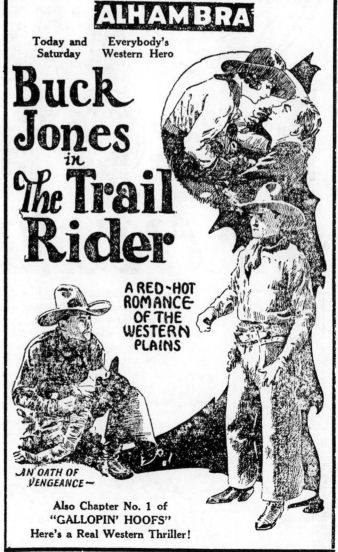

ALHAMBRA

Today and   Everybody's
Saturday   Western Hero

Buck
Jones
in
The Trail
Rider

A RED-HOT
ROMANCE
OF THE
WESTERN
PLAINS

*AN OATH OF
VENGEANCE—*

Also Chapter No. 1 of
"GALLOPIN' HOOFS"
Here's a Real Western Thriller!

RAH! RAH! RAH

He's Here!

HAROLD LLOYD

in

"The Freshman"

JUST THE GOAT OF THE COLLEGE

WHO LONGED FOR GRIDIRON GLORIES AND POPULARITY

BUT ONLY ONE PERSON UNDERSTOOD

Now Breaking Every Motion Picture Attendance Record on *Broadway*

He was welcome! Just like "W-E-L-C-O-M-E" is written on a doormat! For that's just what he was, poor Harold, the doormat of the college! Laughed at! Ridiculed!—Water boy for the team and thinking he was a player—but his chance had come! He was in the game! On the team at last! Or **under** it! They might break his heart, but they could not crush his spirit!

The Picture That Has Caused a New Medical Term to Be Coined Called —LAUGH MADNESS—

ADDED NOVELTY
The FRESHMAN FOUR
COLLEGIATE FAVORITES IN
"Campus Memories"

AESOP'S
FABLES

FIGHTING
HEARTS

PLAY
BALL

Richard
Barthelmess

in

SHORE
LEAVE

He's a
Jackie in
the Navy
with
Sweethearts
in Every
Port

First
National
Pictures

There's not a dull
moment in the life of
the
PRAIRIE
WIFE

A
Romance of
the Plains

She followed the call
of her mate from a
world of pleasure and
fashion into a land
of brute force and
struggle! A picture
of thrills and adven-
ture!

with

Herbert Rawlinson
Dorothy Devore

directed by
Hugo Ballin

from the story by
Arthur Stringer

A Metro-Goldwyn Picture
Also
"Gallopin Hoofs" No. 6
and
Lloyd Hamilton
in
"Crushed"

COOLER HERE THAN ANYWHERE

NEW THEATRE

OUT WHERE THE
THRILLS BEGIN!

ZANE GREY'S smash-
ing romance of the
Arizona border in the days
when a quick trigger and a
fast horse were a man's
best friends.

Outspeeds, outthrills, out-
shines in every way all
Western romance pictures
of the past.

GREATER
MOVIE SEASON
STARTS AUG. 3
AUSPICES
MOTION PICTURE THEATRE
OWNERS OF MARYLAND

—WITH—
JACK
HOLT
NOAH
BEERY
BILLIE
DOVE

a
Paramount
Picture

ZANE
GREY'S
THE
LIGHT OF
WESTERN STARS

Feature Starts:
10.32, 12.20 A. M.,
2.17, 4.12, 6.00,
7.57, 10.00 P. M.

Comedy,
"HOT AND HEAVY."
New Theatre Orchestra
V. Nessul Conducting

87

LON CHANEY
in
"The PHANTOM OF THE OPERA"
with
NORMAN KERRY
and MARY PHILBIN
Heading a Cast of 5,000 Supporting Players
GASTON LEROUX'S Immortal Classic Rendered
On a Scale of Unparalleled Magnificence.

MADISON
TODAY—TUESDAY—WEDNESDAY
MILTON SILLS
in
A BIG
THRILLING
ROMANCE
OF COPS
AND
CUPIDS
The Making of O'Malley
WITH
Dorothy Mackaill

ADDED
News
Mack
Sennett
Comedy

FIRST NATIONAL PICTURES

RUDOLPH VALENTINO
"THE EAGLE"
with VILMA BANKY
LOUISE DRESSER

THE whole town's watching the wooing of Rudy and Vilma! Every critic says it's Valentino's greatest picture! This dashing, heart-stealing Robin Hood has stolen Chicago's heart. Whether you are a Valentino fan or not, see "The Eagle"—it is romantic adventure soaring to the heights!

And, ah! such moments as you'll spend with the naughty Czarina (Louise Dresser), slyly, but not shyly, seeking Rudy's arms!

BALABAN & KATZ
Roosevelt
STATE ST. NEAR WASHINGTON

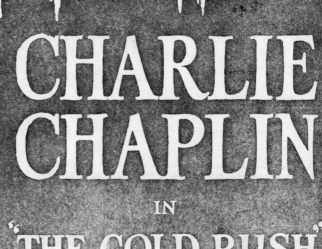

CHARLIE CHAPLIN

IN

"THE GOLD RUSH"

*A Dramatic Comedy
written and directed
by Charlie Chaplin*

"Gold Rush" Breaks Records of 17 Years

"Charlie Chaplin's 'The Gold Rush' broke all records since this house was opened seventeen years ago," telegraphed Aaron Jones, of Jones, Linick and Schaeffer, to Hiram Abrams, president of United Artists Corporation, when this new Chaplin dramatic comedy opened at the Orpheum theatre, Chicago. "All I can say is that it is marvelous. Congratulations."

NOW BOOKING
UNITED ARTISTS CORPORATION
Mary Pickford   Charles Chaplin
Douglas Fairbanks   D. W. Griffith
Hiram Abrams, President   Joseph M. Schenck, Chairman, Board of Directors.

Mystery! Thrills! Romance!
LON CHANEY
in
The Unholy Three

THOMAS MEIGHAN IN
"TONGUES OF FLAME"
A JOSEPH HENABERY PRODUCTION
A Paramount Picture

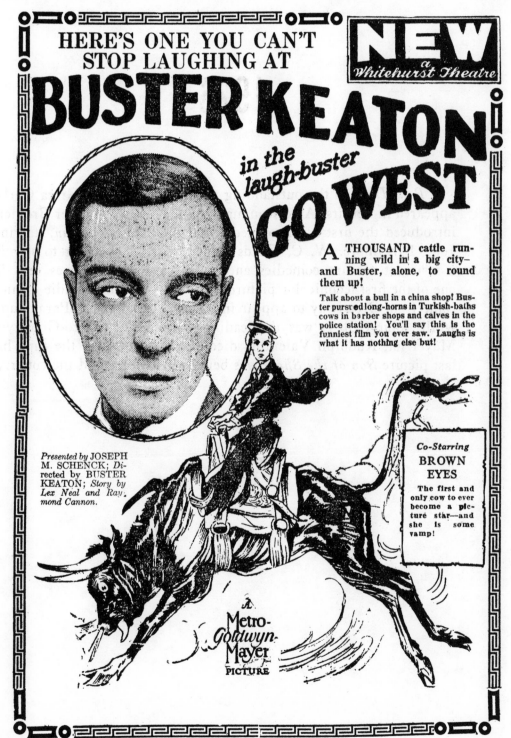

HERE'S ONE YOU CAN'T
STOP LAUGHING AT

NEW
a
Whitehurst Theatre

BUSTER KEATON

in the
laugh-buster
GO WEST

A THOUSAND cattle running wild in a big city—and Buster, alone, to round them up!

Talk about a bull in a china shop! Buster pursued long-horns in Turkish-baths cows in barber shops and calves in the police station! You'll say this is the funniest film you ever saw. Laughs is what it has nothing else but!

Presented by JOSEPH M. SCHENCK; Directed by BUSTER KEATON; Story by Lex Neal and Raymond Cannon.

Co-Starring
BROWN EYES

The first and only cow to ever become a picture star—and she is some vamp!

A
Metro-Goldwyn-Mayer
PICTURE

1926

Ben Hur was the outstanding picture of the year. Greta Garbo appeared in her first American made film, *Torrent*. Warner Brothers introduced the first synchronized-sound picture, *Don Juan,* starring John Barrymore. W. C. Fields signed with Paramount to star in a series of feature comedies and Douglas Fairbanks was seen in one of the first technicolor pictures, *The Black Pirate*. Eddie Cantor came from Broadway to appear in several comedies for Paramount, while John Gilbert was the leading star on the Metro-Goldwyn-Mayer lot. Rudolph Valentino died on August 23, at the time his last picture *Son of the Sheik* was being released around the country.

MONDAY, TUESDAY and WEDNESDAY
REGINALD DENNY
"ROLLING HOME"

NORMA SHEARER
in a picture of
love, laughs, thrills
His Secretary
A Metro-Goldwyn-Mayer PICTURE

—the Flapper was 1923
—the MODERN is 1926!

And chic and charming Colleen gives a version that will last till the year 2000.

COLLEEN MOORE

IN

We Moderns

FIRST NATIONAL PICTURES

Adapted from
Israel Zangwill's Stage Success

The big play of the season which bows out the flapper and bows in the modern.

Directed by the Man Who Made "THE PERFECT FLAPPER"

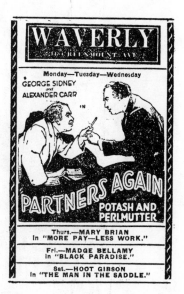

WAVERLY
GREENMOUNT AVE.

Monday—Tuesday—Wednesday
GEORGE SIDNEY
and
ALEXANDER CARR
IN
PARTNERS AGAIN
with POTASH AND PERLMUTTER

Thurs.—MARY BRIAN
In "MORE PAY—LESS WORK."

Fri.—MADGE BELLAMY
In "BLACK PARADISE."

Sat.—HOOT GIBSON
In "THE MAN IN THE SADDLE."

APOLLO Cont. 11 to 11
NOW PLAYING
Richard Barthelmess
in
RANSON'S FOLLY

From the Story by Richard Harding Davis, with
DOROTHY MACKAILL

APOLLO

One Week
Starting
Sunday

The
Love Story
of a Bold
Buccaneer

DOUGLAS FAIRBANKS
in "The Black Pirate"

The Adventure of a Lifetime!

A whoop-'em-up, soaked in the sea, buccaneering yarn, with love and vivid romance always present.

Come and live those pirate dreams of long ago. Come and see The Black Pirate capture a merchant ship single-handed to win his spurs.

Yo! Ho! All ye from 7 to 70 renew your youth and be a pirate bold!

Photographed in Technicolor

WILLIAM FOX Presents

Buck Jones
in
The Gentle Cyclone

Coming

GENE TUNNEY

formidable heavyweight, loser of only one battle and that way back in 1922, in a

Pathéserial

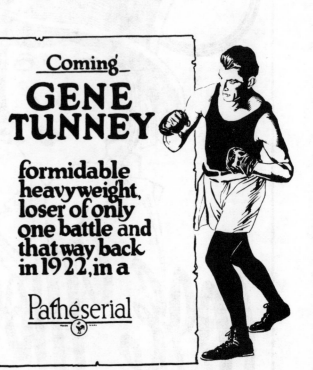

94

APOLLO

ALL WEEK
STARTING TODAY

HIS LATEST AND LAST PICTURE

First Showing in Illinois Outside of Chicago

**A HEART BREAKER!
A RECORD BREAKER!**

RUDOLPH VALENTINO
in
"The Son of the Sheik"
with VILMA BANKY

Riding like the wind! Fighting like a Bedouin, this fiery Son of the Sheik burst in upon them and before their very eyes snatched Yasmin, dancing girl, the toast of the desert, and was away before one hand could stop him.

Ah! Here is Romance here is love such as only Valentino can portray it. Here is a Son of the Sheik who is a greater master than was his father before him.

An eye feast of virile action, colorful settings and glowing climaxes.

The Sequel to "The Sheik"

READ WHAT THE LOS ANGELES NEWSPAPERS SAY ABOUT "THE SON OF THE SHEIK."

100%
entertainment

Coming
NEXT Sunday

An ALLAN DWAN Production
Rex Beach's
Padlocked
with
LOIS MORAN
LOUISE DRESSER
NOAH BEERY
A Paramount Picture

"The Valentino picture for which the world's wife, mother and daughter have been waiting."
(Louella O. Parsons—Examiner)

"The debut of the Sheik's offspring celebrated with acclaim."
(Edwin Schallert—Times)

"Makes the July weather seem frigid for, ooh, such love-making."
(Eleanor Barnes—News)

"Notable for its beauty—first-rate feature."
(Monroe Lathrop—Express)

"Valentino does magnificently."
(Guy Price—Herald)

AT LAST!
HER UTMOST!

*The Ultra
in
Screen
Entertainment*

RIVOLI

FIRST NATIONAL PICTURES

Norma Talmadge
in "KIKI"

—With—
RONALD COLMAN
Based on the stage play "Kiki"—written by
Andre Picard and adapted by David Belasco

You'll Love Kiki—You Can't Help It!

Because Kiki Is Norma Talmadge—
and Norma Talmadge Is Kiki

—COMEDY—

Mack Sennett PRESENTS

BEN TURPIN
"A Prodigal Bridegroom"

RIVOLI SYMPHONY ORCHESTRA. FELICE IULA Conducting

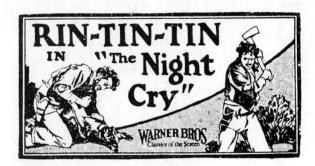

LOEW'S AND UNITED ARTISTS'

VALENCIA

LEXINGTON ST. — ATOP — CONTINUOUS
WEST OF CHARLES. THE CENTURY FROM 10 A.M.

BALTIMORE DEMANDS A THIRD WEEK!

A Record-Smashing Event at the Valencia

French / English /
Je vous aime! / I love you!

"The BIG PARADE"

STARRING **JOHN GILBERT** WITH
RENEE ADOREE AND **KARL DANE**
(A METRO-GOLDWYN-MAYER CLASSIC)
AT POPULAR PRICES
WITH ORIGINAL MUSIC AND EFFECTS

REGULAR PERFORMANCES BEGIN AT
11 - 1 - 3.30 - 5.30 - 7.45 - 9.50
GOOD SEATS AT ALL SHOWS
11 TO
12:30 **25¢** 12:30
TO 5 **35¢** 5 TO
CLOSING **60¢**
EXCEPTING SATURDAY AND HOLIDAYS

JACK
DAUGHERTY
AL. WILSON
WORLD'S CHAMPION STUNT FLYER
EILEEN SEDGWICK
"¾ Fighting Ranger"

MADISON

Starting Tomorrow for Four Days

RICHARD DIX
IN

WITH
ESTHER RALSTON
Directed by
FRED NEWMEYER

a
*Paramount
Picture*

PRESENTED BY
ADOLPH ZUKOR
JESSE L. LASKY

A IN'T he hand-
some! Ain't
he grand," sigh the
girlies in the stand.
"Rip him! Trip
him! Smear him
Wow!" shout op-
ponents. Action?
HOW!

THE QUARTERBACK

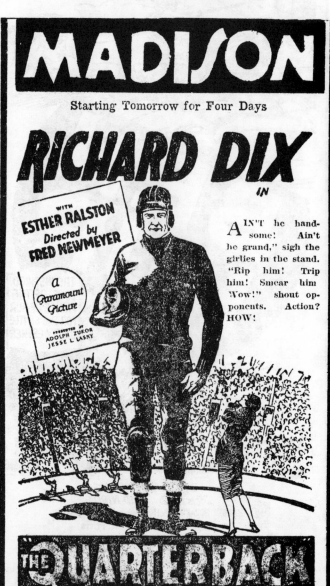

98

WARNER BROS. present

John Barrymore in Don Juan

with MARY ASTOR

ESTELLE TAYLOR — WARNER OLAND
MONTAGU LOVE
HELENE COSTELLO

Directed by ALAN CROSLAND

Scenario by BESS MEREDYTH

A WARNER BROS. PRODUCTION

ZANE GREY'S **FORLORN RIVER**

with

JACK HOLT
RAYMOND HATTON
ARLETTE MARCHAL
EDMUND BURNS

a Paramount Picture

Tom Mix in The CANYON of LIGHT

See the smashing ride of the Vigilantes in the name of law and order — and the terrific fight with blazing guns and fists.

Tonight at 8:30
First Exhibition

twice daily thereafter at 2:30 and 8:30

P. C. Wren's baffling romance of the Sahara. Hard lives, quick deaths, undying love

"Beau Geste"

with

RONALD COLMAN

(by arrangement with Samuel Goldwyn)

A Herbert Brenon Production

Alice Joyce   Mary Brian
Noah Beery   Neil Hamilton
Ralph Forbes   Norman Trevor
William Powell   Victor McLaglen

A Paramount Picture

Presented by
Adolph Zukor and Jesse L. Lasky

Musical presentation by Hugo Riesenfeld

CRITERION

BROADWAY and 44th ST.

BARDELYS' The Magnificent

JOHN GILBERT

Starring
JOHN GILBERT

A GREAT SCREEN ROMANCE

from the Sabatini novel sensation!

KING VIDOR'S Production

ROMANCE! *Adventure! Thrills and heart-throbs!* Here is the picture everyone has been waiting for —the newest triumph of John Gilbert, one of the great lovers of the screen! An epic of love and intrigue, marvelously produced! *Don't miss it!*

with

ELEANOR BOARDMAN
ROY D'ARCY
KARL DANE

A Metro-Goldwyn-Mayer PICTURE

The Picture That Has Caused The Nation To Stare And Gasp In Wonderment---

WILLIAM FOX PRESENTS

3 BAD MEN

Based on Herman Whitaker's novel "OVER the BORDER". The romance of a girl in the land of promise. Civilization marches West. Homeseekers in search of gold, liberty and happiness. Cast of 25,000 with—

GEORGE O'BRIEN
OLIVE BORDEN

J. Farrell MacDonald, Tom Santschi, Frank Campeau, Lou Tellegen, Alec B. Francis, Priscilla Bonner and the Prairie Beauties

JOHN FORD Production

Into a land of terror—a land of gold-maddened men and frenzied women rode a slip of a girl—and 3 BAD MEN.

They were border terrors—killers, who settled disputes with the shooting iron, but they formed a protecting trio for this transplanted desert flower and they rode into eternity with a smile that she might realize the secret of her dreams. It's the mightest of all great dramas of the Early West.

Comedy Attraction
MACK SENNETT
Presents
HARRY
LANGDON
—in—
"SATURDAY
AFTERNOON"

THOMAS MEIGHAN in 'The New Klondike'

a Paramount Picture

WITH LILA LEE

A Florida romance surpassing in background and spectacle the gold rush to the Klondike of old.

From the Story by RING LARDNER

MILTON SILLS in Puppets

They cou'dn't have made it finer—bigger—better. You'll cheer Milton Sills for his wonderful performance.

HAROLD LLOYD

A Paramount Release

in

"FOR HEAVEN'S SAKE!"

Directed by Sam Taylor

Records! Records! RECORDS!

Harold Lloyd's first comedy for Paramount has hit the country like a tornado! Everywhere it's packing more people into theatres than managers ever dreamed four walls could hold!

Produced by HAROLD LLOYD CORPORATION

Laughing
Twinkling
Mischievous
"Mary"
Captivates
New York

Mary Pickford
in "Sparrows"

"Judging by the applause, the laughter, the praise—greatest picture of season."
—Underhill, Herald Tribune

"Our Mary again stirs the heartstrings."
—McGowen, Daily News.

"One of the most captivating of pictures."
—Zimmerman, Telegram.

"A remarkable performance filled with comedy, suspense, action, thrills."
—Stra— Telegraph.

now MARK STRAND
A National Institution
BROADWAY AT 47th STREET
Direction JOSEPH PLUNKETT

MiltonSills
in

The SILENT LOVER

Famous cast. Marvelous desert scenes. Irresistible romance of a Desert Slave Girl and a handsome young Lieutenant who brought her love from another world Presented by First National Pictures, Inc.

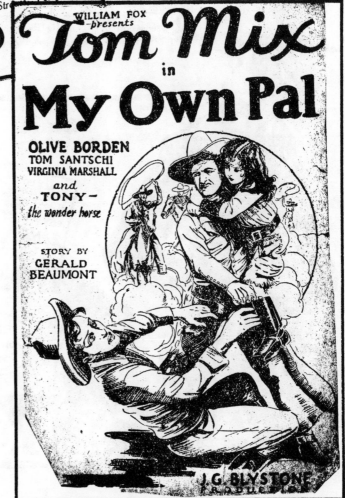

WILLIAM FOX presents
Tom Mix
in
My Own Pal

OLIVE BORDEN
TOM SANTSCHI
VIRGINIA MARSHALL
and
TONY—
the wonder horse

STORY BY
GERALD BEAUMONT

J. G. BLYSTONE
PRODUCTION

JOHNNY HINES
in

The BROWN DERBY

is the speediest comedy made this year—speed boats! speed cars! and a romance that will take your breath away as fast as he took his sweetie's heart away.

THOMAS **MEIGHAN** "IN" **TIN GODS**

NEW *a Whitehurst Theatre*

An ALLAN DWAN Production
—A PARAMOUNT PICTURE—
WITH
RENEE ADOREE
AND
AILEEN PRINGLE

ADDED COMEDY
An Animal Special "Battling Kangaroo"

DRINKING the dregs of the earth and about to strike dead bottom—a cabaret dancer shows him the light. A spectre from the past arrives and then—! Meighan as you've never seen him! Two leading women—Renee Adoree, sensation of "The Big Parade," and Aileen Pringle, regal beauty of the screen.

Starts TODAY!!

JACK HOLT
MARGARET MORRIS
RAYMOND HATTON
ARLETTE MARCHAL
GEORGE SIEGMAN

ZANE GREY'S
"Born to the West"

IF you have red blood in your veins, this picture is for you!

Slam-bang action— Thundering thrills and pleasing romance.

a Paramount Picture

JOHNNY **HINES** IN RAINBOW RILEY
Thurs. Fri. Sat.

APOLLO Continuous 11 to 11

104

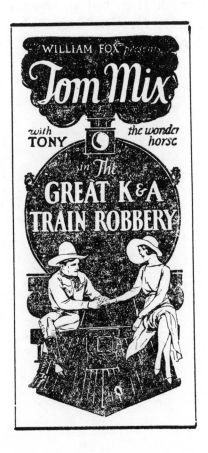

1927

This was the first year of the Academy Awards, the winners being Janet Gaynor for *Seventh Heaven* and Emil Jannings for *The Way of All Flesh*. George Bancroft became a star after his powerful performance in the gangster film *Underworld*, and Clara Bow appeared in *It*, which started her in the sexy comedy-dramas that made her famous. Babe Ruth took time off from hitting home runs for the Yankees to make a baseball picture for First National called *Babe Comes Home*. One of the best pictures of the year was *The General* starring Buster Keaton.

"The best picture ...
MARY has made in
several years" ~says Photoplay Magazine

Mary Pickford in "MY BEST GIRL"

After 3 weeks at RIALTO New York city proves~

NORMA SHEARER

with: LAWRENCE GRAY GWEN LEE

A MONTA BELL production

"AFTER MIDNIGHT"

A METRO-GOLDWYN MAYER PICTURE

HAROLD RAMSAY AT THE ORGAN CONSOLE

*W*HAT happens along Broadway — that glittering garden of gorgeous girls — when midnight strikes? A true story — sheer fascination — Shearer in her most brilliant screen role.

RICHARD Barthelmess

Supported by MOLLY O'DAY and MATHEW BETZ

A Drama that sweeps from a Broadway Honky-Tonk to a frenzy of the Fight Game — to a Living Hell — then back to a Heaven of Happiness these Lovable Lovers never dared hope for.

The PATENT LEATHER KID

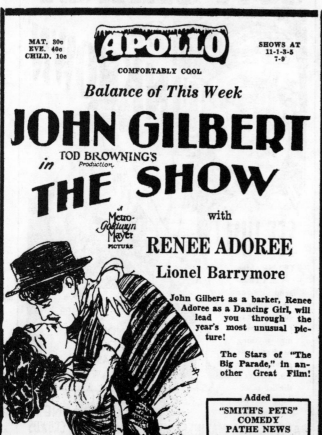

MAT. 30c
EVE. 40c
CHILD. 10c

APOLLO

COMFORTABLY COOL

SHOWS AT 11-1-3-5 7-9

Balance of This Week

JOHN GILBERT

in TOD BROWNING'S Production

THE SHOW

A Metro-Goldwyn Mayer PICTURE

with RENEE ADOREE

Lionel Barrymore

John Gilbert as a barker, Renee Adoree as a Dancing Girl, will lead you through the year's most unusual picture!

The Stars of "The Big Parade," in another Great Film!

Added
"SMITH'S PETS" COMEDY PATHE NEWS

Greatest Comedy Team On the Screen!

GEORGE SIDNEY and CHARLIE MURRAY

First National Pictures

"LOST AT THE FRONT"

Each one a star! Each one good for an evening of laughter! Now you can see them together in one great picture. Twice the laughs! Twice the fun! Twice the comedy of any picture!

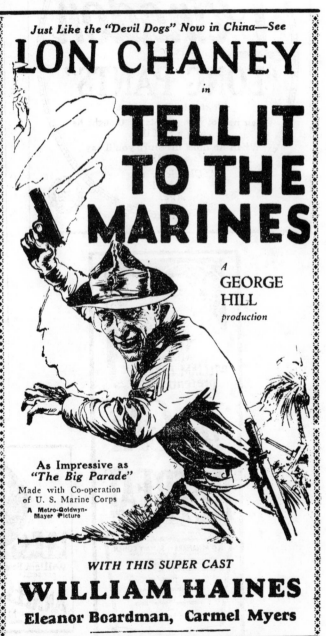

AGAIN!
Another
Smashing
Comedy
Hit!

Harry Langdon

—IN—

"LONG PANTS"

Directed by Frank Capra

When he got Long Pants he thought he was a SHEIK

When he does his stuff you'll say he's a SHRIEK!

A Classic of the Bashful Age!

GLORIA SWANSON

in

The LOVE of SUNYA

Directed by Albert Parker

Glorious Gloria more beautiful, more magnetic, more vivid than ever— in a fiery drama that whirls you with her, searching life's answer to love's questions.

See the new vibrant Gloria in her first United Artists Picture

COMEDY FEATURETTE

MABEL NORMAND in "One Hour Married"

CAST INCLUDES

Creighton Hale & Jimmie Finlayson

Pathécomedy

WILLIAM FOX presents

The GAY RETREAT

A Comedy Classic of War Daze and Parisian Nights with

TED McNAMARA and SAMMY COHEN

THE COMEDY TEAM OF "WHAT PRICE GLORY"

Story by William Conselman and Edward Moran

Adapted by Murray Roth and Edward J. Moran

BEN STOLOFF Production

Laughter! Thrills! Suspense!

Double Barreled Romance!

a story of

American Soldier Boys

and

Loving French Girls

WILLIAM FOX presents

ANKLES PREFERRED

The Intimate story of silk stockings

MADGE BELLAMY

J. FARRELL McDONALD·LAWRENCE GRAY·ALLAN FORREST·BARRY NORTON

New Princess

ALL WEEK

WILLIAM FOX presents

Tom Mix in THE BEST BAD MAN

Newly refurnished. Re-seated. Everything is new. Better class of first run attractions.

112

WILLIAM FOX PRESENTS

What Price Glory

Based on the Stage Triumph *by* Laurence Stallings *and* Maxwell Anderson

As a stage play "What Price Glory" was a sensation. As a motion picture, foremost critics of both stage and screen have unanimously proclaimed it "greater than the play" and one of the great screen masterpieces of all time. Even the piquant atmosphere of this powerful drama—so widely discussed by press and public—has been successfully preserved in the screening.

Up to the present, this spectacular epic in celluloid has been shown only in the large cities. NOW you can see it—in settings more magnificent and effective than would be possible in any stage production, in your own favorite local theatre. Don't miss it! As long as you live you will remember Victor McLaglen as Captain Flagg, and Edmund Lowe as Sergeant Quirt, in their gripping struggle for the love of the beautiful Dolores Del Rio, as the vivacious Charmaine!

This is but one of a succession of superb motion pictures which Fox Film Corporation is now releasing—ambitious pictures—carefully made by great artists—bringing to you all that is finest in screen entertainment.

VICTOR McLAGLEN ⚜ DOLORES DEL RIO ⚜ EDMUND LOWE
RAOUL WALSH
production

THE WORLD'S GREATEST MOTION PICTURE

Come In! Get a Permanent Grin

ADOLPH ZUKOR and JESSE L. LASKY present

W. C. FIELDS

with IVY HARRIS, MARY ALDEN

a Paramount Picture

Directed by FRED NEWMEYER

From the play by J.P. McEVOY

in "THE POTTERS"

Funnier Than "So's Your Old Man!" Don't Miss This!!

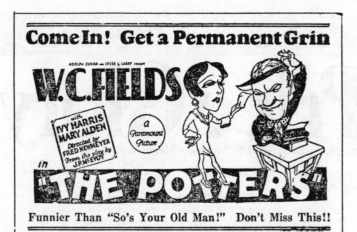

WILLIAM FOX presents

Tom Mix

and TONY the wonder horse

in

The CIRCUS ACE

ALL THE THRILLS OF THE BIG TOP

JOLSON IN THE MOVIES NOW

WARNER BROS. Supreme Triumph!

AL JOLSON in "THE JAZZ SINGER"

NEW SONGS AND OLD FAVORITES SUNG BY MR. JOLSON DURING THE ACTION OF THE STORY ON THE VITAPHONE

A CAST OF EXCEPTIONAL EXCELLENCE HEADED BY MAY McAVOY

WARNER OLAND & CANTOR ROSENBLATT

DIRECTED BY ALAN CROSLAND

Scenario by ALFRED A. COHN

Based upon the play by SAMSON RAPHAELSON as produced on the spoken stage by LEWIS & GORDON and SAM H. HARRIS

NOTE — This Cinema - Vitaphone play depicting the problems of American youth is a pronounced success in New York, Philadelphia, Chicago and other cities where it is playing long runs at advanced prices.

LAUGHS — PATHOS — MELODY

And VITAPHONE Presentations

"When the Wife's Away" With William Demarest

"In a Monastery Cellar" With Gus Reed, Oscar Wahl, Otto Ploetz, Charles Hamilton

A $2.00 ATTRACTION AT REGULAR PRICES!

Richard Barthelmess

in

The DROP Kick

First National Pictures

Emil **JANNINGS**
IN
"THE WAY OF ALL FLESH"
WITH
BELLE BENNETT
And PHYLLIS HAVER—DONALD KEITH
A Paramount Picture

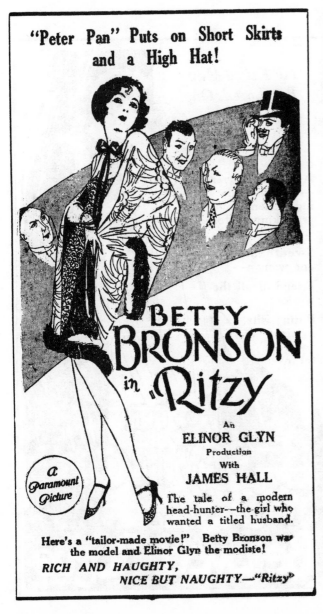

"Peter Pan" Puts on Short Skirts
and a High Hat!

BETTY
BRONSON
in "Ritzy"

An
ELINOR GLYN
Production
With
JAMES HALL

The tale of a modern
head-hunter—the girl who
wanted a titled husband.

Here's a "tailor-made movie!" Betty Bronson was
the model and Elinor Glyn the modiste!
RICH AND HAUGHTY,
NICE BUT NAUGHTY—"Ritzy"

a
Paramount
Picture

If You Enjoy Real Thrills

THEN BY ALL MEANS YOU MUST SEE
WM. HAINES
IN HIS LATEST LAUGHING HIT
"SLIDE,
KELLY,
SLIDE!"

With a Superb Cast, Including
**SALLY O'NEIL
KARL DANE
HARRY CAREY**

What "Brown of Harvard" was
to football, this picture is to
baseball — a whirlwind romance of the grand Amer-
ican game. A sizzling hit
right off the bat; a hilarious tale of pranks,
trials and thrills of
diamond heroes,
with a real love
story.

Including
Actual Scenes
From Great
World Series
Games

A Metro-Goldwyn-
Mayer PICTURE

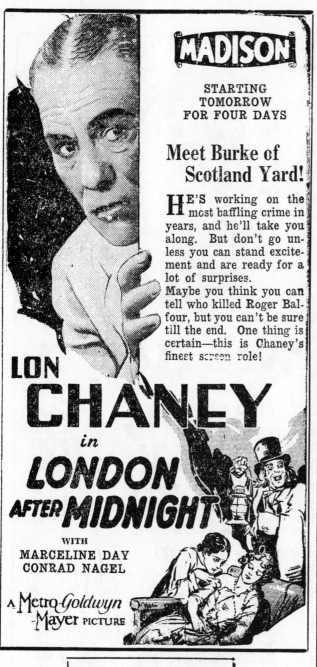

MADISON

STARTING TOMORROW FOR FOUR DAYS

Meet Burke of Scotland Yard!

HE'S working on the most baffling crime in years, and he'll take you along. But don't go unless you can stand excitement and are ready for a lot of surprises.
Maybe you think you can tell who killed Roger Balfour, but you can't be sure till the end. One thing is certain—this is Chaney's finest screen role!

LON CHANEY
in
LONDON AFTER MIDNIGHT

WITH
MARCELINE DAY
CONRAD NAGEL

A Metro-Goldwyn-Mayer PICTURE

WILLIAM FOX presents **Tom Mix** and TONY the wonder horse in **The LAST TRAIL**

EMIL JANNINGS in "The Last Command"

COMEDY—
Charlie Chase
"Never the Dames Shall Meet"

Ken Maynard in The OVERLAND STAGE

First National Pictures

The popular favorite of picture fans—Ken Maynard is back again—now in a picture thrill packed and thoroughly amusing.

He Kissed Many But Loved One!

A care-free lover — fearless, daring, ardent wooer, risking all for stolen kisses.

Sweetheart to one woman—

Friend of all the weak.

Pitting wits against swords for love.

JOHN Barrymore in The Beloved Rogue

DIRECT FROM
Roxy's New Theatre
A TENSE STORY OF ELEMENTAL EMOTIONS

The stark drama of a beautiful Spanish dancing girl, and of a sheep rancher played on the pitiless, super-heated desert—
What was this devoted wife to do? She loved her husband, his father hated her and another man coveted her. The monotony of life on the desert all but drove her mad, and—
A tremendous love theme graphically screened—A great picture with a smashing climax that lifts it into a class all its own.

Produced by
DE MILLE PICTURES CORPORATION

JETTA GOUDAL
in "White Gold"

WITH
KENNETH THOMSON
and
GEORGE BANCROFT

DIRECTED BY
WILLIAM K. HOWARD

Today—Monday—Tuesday

Here it is! Pennant winner of all baseball pictures! World series thrills plus a great romance!

See the greatest diamond star of all time in his first feature film!

FIRST NATIONAL PICTURES

BABE RUTH
in BABE COMES HOME

SEE THIS
SPECIAL PICTURES OF LINDBERGH'S FLIGHT TO PARIS

LADIES!

You'll enjoy "Babe Comes Home" just as much as the menfolks

MADISON
CHILD., 10c   ADULTS 50c
SHOWS 1-3-5-7-9

TODAY--MONDAY--TUESDAY

RAMON NOVARRO

—the star of "Ben-Hur" fights his way to a lovers' Paradise again, in a film crammed with thrills and beauty.

with
ALICE TERRY

in LOVERS

The beautiful wife of his best friend had come to him for help—and then the husband had discovered them!

117

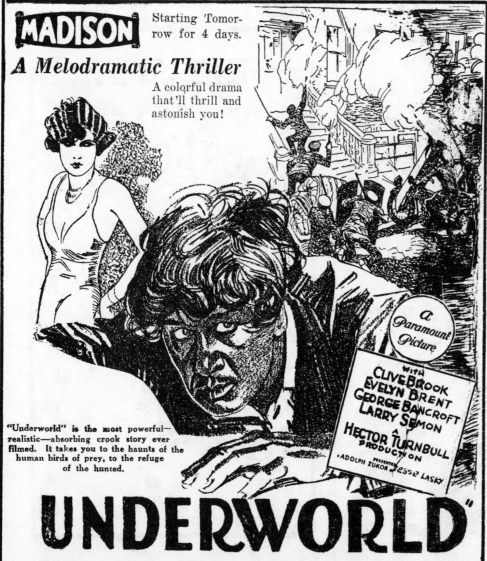

THE TIME OF YOUR LIFE!

A Laugh for Every Tick
of the Clock!

RAYMOND GRIFFITH in **TIME TO LOVE**

With

William Powell   **Vera Voronina**

A Crowded Hour of Girls and Gayety!

A Frank Tuttle Production   A Paramount Picture

IT'S LAUGH WEEK!

Smiles -- Giggles -- Chuckles

LAUGHS--ROARS

EVERYBODY LAUGHS BUT BUSTER!

COME AND SEE

Buster Keaton

IN THE

General

United Artists Picture

His Biggest!
His Funniest!
His Bestest Best!

INSPIRATION PICTURES, INC. presents

RICHARD **BARTHELMESS** in **The White Black Sheep**

With **PATSY RUTH MILLER**

Screen story by VIOLET E. POWELL

A SIDNEY OLCOTT PRODUCTION

A FIRST NATIONAL PICTURE

Barthelmess Fights and Loves in Far-off Lands

The Black Sheep of a noble family—because he wouldn't betray his fiancee!

In the drawing rooms of Europe a girl of society brought him disgrace . . . In the bazaars of the Orient a girl of the gutter saved him from death!

East of Suez . . . Desert mystery . . . Treacherous tribes attacking in the night . . . And only the Black Sheep could ward the blow from those who spurned him!

You'll sit spellbound as Dick Barthelmess builds this film into one solid hour of slashing action—his most adventurous role!

EMPIRE THEATRE

WILLIAM FOX presents

BUCK JONES in DESERT VALLEY

A Thriller of the Sage-Brush Land

with VIRGINIA BROWN FAIRE — MALCOLM WAITE

SCOTT DUNLAP Production

Thrills and Suspense—A Cattlemen's Feud over Water-Rights—And Buck Jones in a story of romance and danger.

ADDED—GUMP COMEDY, "A BIG SURPRISE"

1928

Motion picture theaters throughout the country were being wired for sound as more "part-talking" pictures were released. By the end of the year, the first "all-talking" picture, *Lights of New York,* was seen. Tom Mix ended his long association with William Fox studios and signed for a series of westerns at F.B.O. Pictures. Laurel & Hardy were now the most popular comedy team, and their two-reel comedies, such as *The Finishing Touch* and *Two Tars,* shared equal billing on the marquees of theaters with the feature pictures with which they appeared.

WILLIAM BOYD *IN* "Skyscraper"

WITH
ALAN HALE,
SUE CAROL AND
ALBERTA VAUGHN

WILLIAM BOYD

If you were to tell in detail your idea of your ideal picture you'd be describing something very close to "Skyscraper."

Remembering William Boyd in "The Volga Boatman," "Dress Parade"

Directed by
HOWARD HIGGIN

You'll *love* "Skyscraper." Ask at your local theatre when it will be playing.

A d a p t e d by Elliott Clawson and Tay Garnett from the story by Dudley Murphy.

Pathé
Distributors

DE MILLE
Studio Production

Romance of a Salesgirl and a Salesman on the Road to Happiness.....

WILLIAM FOX presents

MADGE BELLAMY

"SILK LEGS"

JAMES HALL
JOSEPH CAWTHORN
MAUD FULTON
and a Big
Supporting Company
of Beautiful Models

HE'LL SET YOU ON THE EDGE OF YOUR SEAT AND KEEP YOU THERE. A NEW "DIX" YOU'LL LIKE.

Our Gang Comedy "THE OLD WALLOP"

a Paramount Picture

richard DIX in 'the gay defender'

PRINCESS
Today—Ending Thursday

WILLIAM FOX presents ~

Tom Mix
WITH TONY IN ~
The ARIZONA WILDCAT

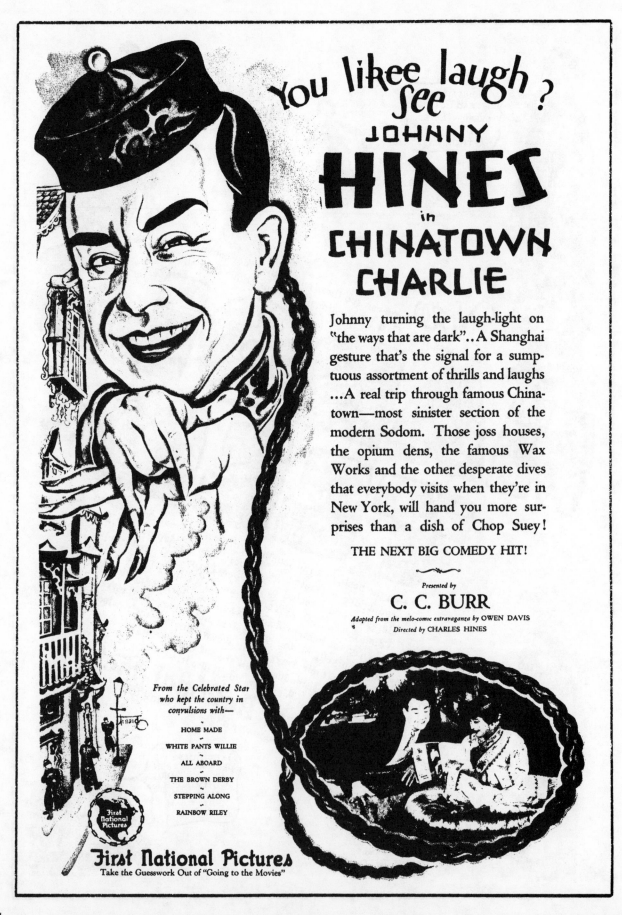

You likee laugh? See
JOHNNY
HINES
in
CHINATOWN
CHARLIE

Johnny turning the laugh-light on "the ways that are dark"..A Shanghai gesture that's the signal for a sumptuous assortment of thrills and laughs ...A real trip through famous Chinatown—most sinister section of the modern Sodom. Those joss houses, the opium dens, the famous Wax Works and the other desperate dives that everybody visits when they're in New York, will hand you more surprises than a dish of Chop Suey!

THE NEXT BIG COMEDY HIT!

Presented by
C. C. BURR
Adapted from the melo-comic extravaganza by OWEN DAVIS
Directed by CHARLES HINES

From the Celebrated Star who kept the country in convulsions with—

HOME MADE

WHITE PANTS WILLIE

ALL ABOARD

THE BROWN DERBY

STEPPING ALONG

RAINBOW RILEY

First National Pictures

First National Pictures
Take the Guesswork Out of "Going to the Movies"

MADISON

Matinee
Child 10c
Adult 30c

Evening
Child 15c
Adult 40c

ALWAYS 70 DEGREES COOL

Four Days, Starting Today!

A TENSE, DRAMATIC STORY OF
THE UPPER AND UNDERWORLD!

RICHARD **BARTHELMESS** in

WHEEL of CHANCE

See drama that you
have never seen be-
fore! See Richard
Barthelmess in
two great char-
acterizations! It's
as powerful as
"The Patent
Leather Kid," as
gripping as "The
Noose."

LEONARD
LEIGH
At the
Hinners
Organ
presents
"CHIQUITA"

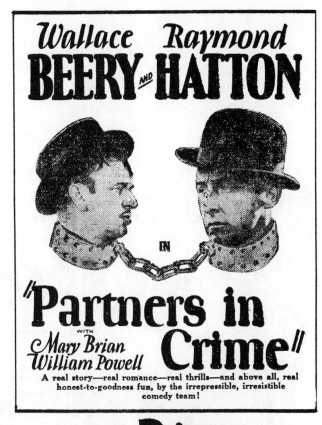

Wallace **BEERY** AND Raymond **HATTON**

IN

"Partners in Crime"

WITH
Mary Brian
William Powell

A real story—real romance—real thrills—and above all, real
honest-to-goodness fun, by the irrepressible, irresistible
comedy team!

SEE AND
HEAR The **1st "ALL TALKING" PICTURE**

LIGHTS OF NEW YORK

WITH
AN ALL-STAR CAST

STORY BY HUGH HERBERT AND MURRAY ROTH
DIRECTED BY BRYAN FOY

Avoid Night
Crowds
Attend Our
Matinees

HERE'S
THE THRILL
OF YOUR
LIFE

A
WARNER
BROS. **VITAPHONE** PICTURE

4 - ADDED ATTRACTIONS - 4

No. 1 KARYL NORMAN, "The Creole Fashion Plate," the best
female impersonator on the stage.

No. 2 SHAW and LEE, the "Beau Brummels" a happy and
hilarious couple.

BEBE DANIELS

IN **"HOT NEWS"**

READ on. Bebe
is the only come-
dienne on the screen
today who can at the
same time supply
laughs and "It"—the
combination you
can't resist.

HERE she is
again in a brand
new series of stunt
thrills that enliven
all her pictures.

WITH
NEIL HAMILTON

REALLY
REFRIGERATED
ALWAYS
DELIGHTFUL

ON THE STAGE
Buddy Page
Our New Bandmaster
of Ceremonies
Presenting
"IT MIGHT HAPPEN"
With
Cozert and Mottu
Reckless Recco
Billy Roles
Grace
Johnson
Dolores
8 Ada Kaufman Girls
and the
Stanley Stage Band
A Stanley Revue

FLAMING LOVE

CAUGHT IN THE SWIRL OF PASSION AND SACRIFICE!

the stars of "Flesh and the Devil" *together again!*

While New York Is Fighting To See "Love," Paying $2.00 Admission, See It Here At Regular Prices

JOHN **GILBERT** GRETA **GARBO**

in

LOVE

A STORY of love—*but what a story!*

Love triumphant over suffering and disaster, love smiling pitiably through heartbreak!

A surging romance—from Tolstoi's immortal novel—with the brilliant stars of "Flesh and the Devil."

THE YEAR'S SCREEN EVENT!

METRO-GOLDWYN MAYER PICTURE

FLIES TO FRANCE *to find* ROMANCE!

Over the Sea~ Like our own Lindy **MONTE BLUE** IN "ACROSS THE ATLANTIC"

WITH **EDNA MURPHY**

A WARNER BROS. PRODUCTION

A vivid drama of Gypsy life and love!

Columbia Pictures *presents*

JACK HOLT

in

"THE TIGRESS"

With **DOROTHY REVIER**

You'll forget that it's a picture and live and breath with Mona, the wild creature of the wilderness. You'll love with her—laugh with her and cry with her. You'll mingle the bitter with the sweet and leave the theatre feeling you have left a friend behind.

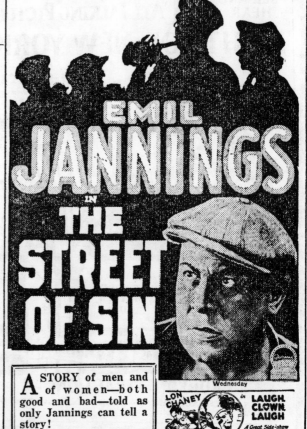

EMIL JANNINGS

in

THE STREET OF SIN

A STORY of men and of women—both good and bad—told as only Jannings can tell a story!

Wednesday

LON CHANEY *in* LAUGH CLOWN LAUGH

A Great Side-show of Life!

126

The "LAUGH SPECIAL"
"Honey"---Turned to "Alim---oney"!
"Dearie"---Turned to "De---cree"!

Marie *Prevost*

RENO---
the haven of those who take off their shoes when they take out their latch-keys— America's divorce Mecca—a city that welcomes all who seek to cast off the shackles of misfit matrimony—a comedy vibrant with drama, thrills and wholesome laughs.

A Pathe De Mille Production

in "ON TO RENO"

VILMA
MAYFIELD AVE. & BELAIR RD.

Monday
Marion DAVIES
THE PATSY

Tuesday
BILLIE DOVE
—THE HEART OF A FOLLIES GIRL

Wednesday and Thursday
DOLORES COSTELLO
IN "TENDERLOIN"
with CONRAD NAGEL
MITCHELL LEWIS — DAN WOLHEIM
JOHN MILJAN — GEORGIE STONE

FRIDAY AND SATURDAY
ZANE GREYS "THE WATER HOLE"
with Jack Holt — Nancy Carroll

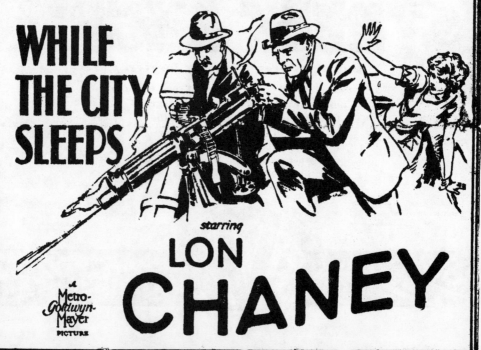

APOLLO
A "GREAT STATES" THEATRE
THURSDAY--FRIDAY
SATURDAY

Chaney's Finest Underworld Film!

BROUGHT BACK BY POPULAR DEMAND
Detectives, the underworld, thrills—and a glorious romance. Here is the real "inside" story of how New York plainclothesmen battle the forces of crime by day and by night.

WHILE THE CITY SLEEPS

starring
LON CHANEY

A Metro-Goldwyn-Mayer PICTURE

"WINGS"

WITH
CLARA
BOW
CHARLES (Buddy)
ROGERS
RICHARD
ARLEN
GARY
COOPER

a

DARING danger and
destruction. Scouring
the skies for enemy planes.
Soaring to the clouds in a
flimsy machine.
And yet, like a charm,
her love kept this "Shooting Star." Carried him
through the terrific dangers.
Brought him back to earth.
Spirited, striving, spectacular. A story of the American war "Aces" in France.

Paramount
Picture

A LUCIEN HUBBARD PRODUCTION   DIRECTED BY WILLIAM A. WELLMAN

HAROLD LLOYD in "SPEEDY"

produced by Harold Lloyd Corp.
a Paramount Release

"best show in town"

a horse car load of laughs

Let's have fun!
All out to see Harold Lloyd in his latest picture ... "Speedy!" He's New York's mile-a-minute, smile-a-minute kid ... jumping from one job to another and one laugh to another. Ask your Theatre Manager for the date!

Ask your Theatre Manager for the dates of *all* the great Paramount Pictures of 1928—"Gentlemen Prefer Blondes", Emil Jannings in "The Last Command", "Tillie's Punctured Romance", "Legion of the Condemned"—everyone is sure to be the *"best show in town"*.

PARAMOUNT FAMOUS LASKY CORP.
Adolph Zukor, Pres., Paramount Bldg., N. Y.
"If it's a Paramount Picture, it's the best show in town"

Paramount Pictures

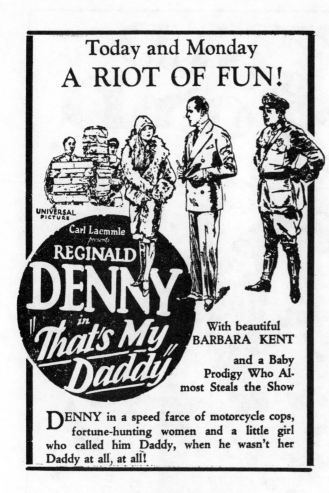

Today and Monday
A RIOT OF FUN!

UNIVERSAL PICTURE

Carl Laemmle
presents

REGINALD
DENNY
in
"That's My
Daddy"

With beautiful
BARBARA KENT

and a Baby
Prodigy Who Almost Steals the Show

DENNY in a speed farce of motorcycle cops,
fortune-hunting women and a little girl
who called him Daddy, when he wasn't her
Daddy at all, at all!

VIVID! SENSATIONAL!
GEORGE
BANCROFT
"The Drag Net"
WITH
EVELYN BRENT
WILLIAM POWELL
A Paramount Picture

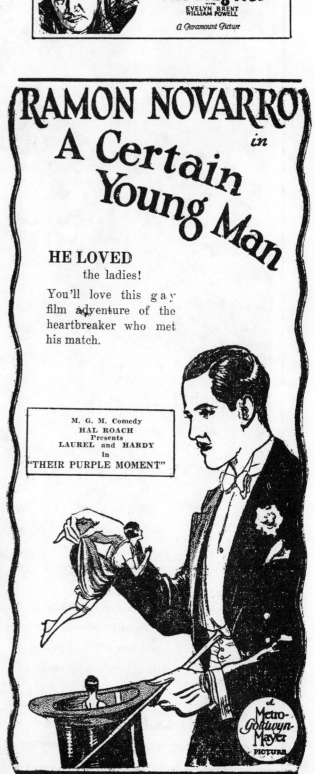

RAMON NOVARRO
in
A Certain
Young Man

HE LOVED
the ladies!

You'll love this gay
film adventure of the
heartbreaker who met
his match.

M. G. M. Comedy
HAL ROACH
Presents
LAUREL and HARDY
in
"THEIR PURPLE MOMENT"

A
Metro-
Goldwyn-
Mayer
PICTURE

"DOUGLAS
FAIRBANKS
as
"The GAUCHO"

BILLY DOOLEY

HE may not be much of a seaman, but as a comic he's hard to beat—Billy Dooley —saltiest sailor of them all, afloat or ashore! Waves of laughter and oceans of fun in every one of his Paramount-Christie comedies— "Easy Curves," "Dizzy Sights," "Water Bugs." See them at best theatres everywhere.

Paramount-Christie Comedies

1929

Harold Lloyd was successful with his first talking picture *Welcome Danger* and Douglas Fairbanks talked in the prologue of his first sound picture *The Iron Mask*. Ronald Colman became one of the most popular stars in talking pictures because of his fine voice and perfect diction, which came from his earlier years on the stage. Mary Pickford won the Academy Award for her performance in *Coquette* and Warner Baxter was the male winner for his role as the "Cisco Kid" in the first outdoor talking picture, *In Old Arizona*. At this time Gary Cooper and Richard Arlen appeared in their first all-talking picture, *The Virginian*.

Who
killed Broadway's most beautiful show girl?

Was it Dr. Lindquist, who loved her?

Was it Louis Mannix, who feared her?

Was it Charles Spotswoode, who hated her?

Was it Jim Spotswoode, afraid of her?

Was it Charles Cleaver, blackmailed by her?

Was it Tony Skeel, who sought her jewels?

HEAR and SEE PARAMOUNT'S thrilling ALL-TALKING picturization of the most popular mystery-detective novel in the past ten years. Directed by Malcolm St. Clair with

WILLIAM POWELL as PHILO VANCE and a great cast including Louise Brooks and James Hall.

A PARAMOUNT ALL TALKING PICTURE

LOUIS MANNIX

CHARLES SPOTSWOODE

DR. LINDQUIST

JIMMIE SPOTSWOODE

TONY SKEEL

CHARLES CLEAVER

THE CANARY MURDER CASE
A PHILO VANCE STORY

PHILO VANCE
SEE and HEAR William Powell as the world's greatest detective solve this mystery in a dramatic thrilling manner.

LEADER
SOUND AND SILENT

"THE CANARY MURDER CASE"

The TALKING PICTURE REACHES PERFECTION
IN OLD ARIZONA

"I can have any man I want" said Tonia Hear *and* See what happened to the girl who boasted she could get her man!

Actually filmed and recorded *on location* IN OLD ARIZONA represents a distinct forward step in the art of the talking picture. For the first time, WILLIAM FOX brings to the screen not only the realistic settings but also the *natural sounds* of the great outdoors! The voices you hear are voices as they really sound *out in the open!* Until you've seen and heard IN OLD ARIZONA you can't appreciate to what heights the technique of the talking motion picture has been advanced by Fox Movietone! Keep abreast of developments in this newest field of expression—make up your mind to see IN OLD ARIZONA when it comes to your favorite local theater.

Every part is a *speaking* part— featured in the leading roles are two brilliant screen stars and a fascinating stage favorite — EDMUND LOWE as Sgt. Dunn, the heartbreaking cavalryman; WARNER BAXTER as the Cisco Kid, outlawed Don Juan of the desert; and, in her first screen appearance, DOROTHY BURGESS as Tonia, the fiery, fickle, light-o-love who pays the price of infidelity in one of the most startling denouements ever filmed! In the supporting roles are nearly a score of well-known players of the stage and screen. With such a cast under the masterful direction of Raoul Walsh and Irving Cummings it is no wonder audiences everywhere have acclaimed IN OLD ARIZONA as one of the *great* pictures of the year!

FOX MOVIETONE

DOUGLAS FAIRBANKS
AS D'ARTAGNAN IN
The IRON MASK
DIRECTED BY
ALLAN DWAN
UNITED ARTISTS PICTURE

THE FURTHER
ADVENTURES
OF THE
THREE
MUSKETEERS

THE ULTRA OF SOUND PERFECTION

The Original
"Jazz Singer"
In His First
Talking and
Singing
Production

Tiffany-
Stahl
Presents

GEORGE JESSEL IN "Lucky Boy"

From the Story
By Viola Brothers Shore

*Musical Score by
Hugo Reisenfeld*

SEE AND HEAR!
The Greatest of All Air
Pictures—

THE
STAR OF
"BEN HUR"
IN
ANOTHER
EPIC!

**RAMON
NOVARRO**
IN
**THE
FLYING
FLEET**

—WITH—
**ANITA PAGE
RALPH GRAVES
EDWARD NUGENT**
Dedicated to the Heroic Fliers
of the U. S. Navy
—and—

4 Superb "Talkie" Acts

**VINCENT LOPEZ
CHAZ CHASE
SHAW ANOLEE
ELSA ERSI & NAT AYER**

NOW!
Come
Early!
11 to 1
35c

*He played at
love as a
thrilling game
...To her...
love was the
most beauti-
ful thing in
life....*

You'll thrill to every moment of this great Para-
mount New Show World
Sensation . . . .

ALL·TALKING

**"BEHIND the
MAKEUP"**
with
WILLIAM POWELL
FAY WRAY · HAL SKELLY
ADDED
"He Loved the Ladies"
Yacht Club Boys
"Marriage Wows"
Paramount News

"The Home of
Paramount
Pictures"

FREE!
The first 300 ladies
attending matinees
will receive Max
Factor cosmetics
courtesy of Fay Wray.

Royal Theater Park-
ing Service at 9th
and Main Garage...
3 hours for 15c.

ROYAL
1022 MAIN ST.

THE UNHOLY NIGHT

A Metro-
Goldwyn-
Mayer
ALL
TALKING
PICTURE

A perfectly done mystery
thriller comes now to the
Talking Screen.

Suspense, terror, blended with
romance — here is entertainment you've been waiting for.

with

**ERNEST
TORRENCE**

**DOROTHY
SEBASTIAN**

**ROLAND
YOUNG**

directed by
**LIONEL
BARRYMORE**

WILLIAM HAINES IN ALIAS JIMMY VALENTINE

with
LIONEL BARRYMORE — KARL DANE — LEILA HYAMS

A Jack Conway Production
From the play by
Paul Armstrong
Adaptation by A. P. Younger
Continuity by
Sara Y. Mason
Titles by Joe Farnham

JIMMY GETS
THE THIRD DEGREE

Slowly . . . silently . . . ominously . . . the great steel door swung shut, locking within that airless vault a helpless little child—the sister of the girl he loved . . .

He had endured the third degree—could he stand that pitiful appeal? To "crack" the safe was a confession—not to, was—murder! What did "Jimmy Valentine" decide?

It's an evening you'll remember all your life. A smash hit on Broadway at $2 admission acclaimed the perfected dialogue accompaniment. You'll have all the same thrills when your local theatre shows this record-breaking Metro-Goldwyn-Mayer film, either silent or with dialogue.

THE CONSPIRATORS
WILLIAM HAINES — KARL DANE — TULLY MARSHALL

Paramount's star in his first ALL TALKING Comedy

RICHARD DIX

with HELEN KANE Broadway's latest craze, in

"NOTHING BUT the TRUTH"

Haven't you often wondered what Dix's voice sounds like?
Hear it in Wm. Collier's Most Laughable Stage Romance of Complications Ever Brought to the Screen.

HEAR HELEN KANE
Sing "Do Something"

More mysterious, more gripping than "Canary Murder Case"

THE GREENE MURDER CASE

Paramount's ALL TALKING Detective Tale by S. S. Van Dyne

WM. POWELL as PHILO VANCE, Society Detective

WILLIE AND EUGENE HOWARD On Singing Screen

On the Stage
'VICTOR HERBERT'S MELODIES"
Chorus Ballet
Orchestral gem, "William Tell"

VICTORIA

THIS WEEK ONLY

No Increase
In Prices.
A Paramount
All-Talking
Picture.

Two things he loved

...The Race For Gold...The Arms of His Beautiful Wife

:.. and while he fought for money in the roaring battle of Wall Street, that lovely creature he thought was his, sought the arms of another.

Don't miss this exciting ALL-TALK-ING PARAMOUNT PICTURE. HEAR the rush and roar of Wall Street, SEE the battle-ground of the money giants; the frenzied excitement of the Stock Exchange, real, nerve-tingling, fascinating! SEE George Bancroft as the towering figure of finance. HEAR the seductive Baclanova as his enticing wife, cajoling, pleading, enmeshing the wizard of wealth in her silken web.

A terrific drama of power, wealth, and love! Directed by ROWLAND V. LEE with Baclanova and Nancy Carroll.

PARAMOUNT PRESENTS THE GREATEST ALL-TALKING PICTURE YET PRODUCED!

GEORGE BANCROFT *in* THE WOLF OF WALL STREET"

Now HEAR Harold Lloyd in his first talking picture!

You'd think he couldn't possibly be any funnier, but you'll *hear* he is when you see him in "Welcome Danger," his first sound and dialog picture. *Twice* the laughs than ever before, if you can imagine *that!* ❦ You'll be all eyes and ears when you see it—it has laughs, thrills, romance, youth, gayety, *everything!* And what a treat for the children—more fun than a three-ringed circus. ❦ Don't miss seeing and hearing Harold Lloyd in "Welcome Danger" when it comes to your theatre. You'll laugh at every minute of it, and it will give you something to talk about for weeks after!

HAROLD LLOYD
IN "WELCOME DANGER"

Produced by the Harold Lloyd Corporation. A Paramount Sound and Dialog Release.

LON CHANEY in "Thunder" with PHYLLIS HAVER JAMES MURRAY

TO-DAY PALACE
11 a.m., 1—3—5—7 & 9 p.m.

ROD LA ROCQUE
IN "BEAU BANDIT"
All-TALKING OUTDOOR THRILLER

MAN ABOUT TOWN Silent Comedy	HOLDING HIS OWN Silent Comedy

Radio PICTURES

PRICES:
P0.30 | P0.70

now it's on the screen—with talking, singing and sound!

❆ Thrill to the magnificent voice of Jean Hersholt! ❆ Hear Nancy Carroll as she sings, while Charles Rogers accompanies her on the piano!

THE wonder play that shattered every record in theatrical history, greater than ever as a Paramount Picture — all its laughs, thrills, tears . . . intensified a hundredfold! Something you must see and are sure to enjoy, "silent" or with sound. ❆ Only an organization commanding the resources of Paramount could first of all secure this most valuable property, and then make it even greater as a motion picture than it was as a play! ❆ "Silent" or with Sound, "if it's a Paramount Picture it's the best show in town!"

ANNE NICHOLS' "ABIE'S IRISH ROSE"

With Jean Hersholt, Charles Rogers and Nancy Carroll. A Victor Fleming Production.

And watch for!
"INTERFERENCE"
The first QUALITY All-Talking Picture

◆

Emil Jannings in
"SINS OF THE FATHERS"

◆

"THE CANARY MURDER CASE"
With Sound and Dialog

◆

"THE CASE OF LENA SMITH"
Starring Esther Ralston

◆

Richard Dix in
"REDSKIN"
Sound and Technicolor

Hailed as a hero.... then hurled into disgrace!

See Richard Dix, greater than he was in the Vanishing American, as a redman's chief . . an outcast from his tribe, fighting his way to wealth and love!

See this dynamic drama filmed in gorgeous NATURAL COLORS. New York paid $2. to see this sensational spectacle and they're still raving about it. It has everything! The mysterious Navajo country actually filmed in NATURAL COLORS; a wonderful love story; heart stirring pathos . . . and action. What action! College triumphs; fierce tribal hatreds; the greed for gold! The rush for oil; stirring combat; thrilling chases over mountain and desert. It's a knockout! The amazing COLOR photography is worth the price of admission alone. Don't miss

RICHARD DIX
IN "REDSKIN"

PARAMOUNT'S SENSATIONAL SPECTACLE IN SOUND AND COLOR THAT NEW YORK PAID $2.00 TO SEE.

Next Week No Increase In Prices

DWARFS THE STAGE

with its perfect presentation of one of the theatre's great masterpieces!

GEORGE ARLISS *in* "DISRAELI"

If you have cheers, prepare to give them now. For with George Arliss in "Disraeli" the art of Talking Pictures enters a new phase!

Experts have been predicting that it would take ten years to perfect the audible film. The experts were wrong! For here is that perfection, achieved by *Vitaphone* years ahead of time!

Not only has *Vitaphone* transplanted every atom of dramatic power, superb suspense, and rapier

wit, that made George Arliss' "Disraeli" one of the historic stage successes of the century... It has done *more* than that ... In a single stride it has not only attained but actually *surpassed* the stage's artistic standards, which thousands felt the screen could never even equal!

The fascination of the footlights

"Vitaphone" is the registered trade mark of the Vitaphone Corporation

fades before the larger lure of mammoth settings—Vitaphone's crisp, telling dialogue—and a George Arliss of heightened stature and new intimacy, exceeding even the amazing brilliance of his classic stage performance.

Come! See for yourself! Let *Vitaphone* put you "on speaking terms" with Disraeli, amazing man of destiny who rose from obscurity to control a modern empire—all because he knew how to handle women—especially a Queen.

WILLIAM FOX *presents*
SALUTE
with
GEORGE O'BRIEN
HELEN CHANDLER
Directed by
JOHN FORD
ALL TALKING
Movietone

PARAMOUNT'S QUALITY ALL-TALKING SHOW

"So remarkable that it changes the opinion of countless sceptics concerning talking films."

New York Times

Unit One

The first great quality all-talking motion picture. From the sensational stage success that ran over a year on Broadway. ℂ A gripping melodrama of the upperworld with complete dialogue throughout — not a silent scene in it. Directed by Roy J. Pomeroy from the stage play by Roland Pertwee and Harold Dearden with

EVELYN BRENT
DORIS KENYON
CLIVE BROOK
WILLIAM POWELL

"INTERFERENCE"

Unit Two

Unit Three

EDDIE CANTOR

(by arrangement with Florenz Ziegfeld, Jr.)

"That Party in Person"

A De-Luxe Singing and Talking Short Feature starring Broadway's dynamic comedian. Hear him—See him do the stuff that makes him such a sensation on Broadway. With pretty Bobbe Arnst, Ziegfeld headliner.

RUTH ETTING

(by arrangement with Florenz Ziegfeld, Jr.)

"The Sweetheart of Song"

Ziegfeld beauty, headliner and Sweetheart of Columbia Records. Hear her jazz over song hits by Irving Berlin and Walter Donaldson, as only she can.

144

UNITED ARTISTS
RANDOLPH ST. at DEARBORN ST

At 9 a. m.—Midnight Show Saturday

THIRD RECORD-BREAKING WEEK OF THRILLS
Ronald COLMAN
Joan Bennett, Lilyan Tashman, Montagu Love—in SAMUEL GOLDWYN'S all-talking romance,

"BULLDOG DRUMMOND"

Colman's voice is the "find" of this all-talking year, rich, humorous, romantic

Extra-Talking Comedy-Scream
Laurel & Hardy in domestic mishap 'PERFECT DAY'

A Smashing, Dashing, Flashing, All-Talking Picture of Love, Adventure, and Daredevil Airmanship!

PATHÉ presents
WILLIAM BOYD

HE FLIRTED WITH DEATH---MADE LOVE IN THE SKY!

the Flying Fool

Thrills Galore!

ALL TALKING epic of the Air

Marie Prevost
Russell Gleason
Tom O'Brien

Coming Wednesday
Victor McLaglen
in "the Black Watch"
ALL-TALKING

METROPOLITAN
NORTH AVE. at PENNSYLVANIA
DIRECTION WARNER EQUITY THEATRES INC.

"Sonny Boy" and His Singing Daddy Are Here Again!

SEE AND HEAR

SEP 9 - 1929

AL JOLSON
IN
"SAY IT WITH SONGS"
WITH
DAVEY LEE
MARIAN NIXON

—With—
Vitaphone Symphony Orchestra

WARNER BROS. & VITAPHONE TALKING PICTURES

Special Vitaphone Presentation
FRANCES SHELLEY
—and—
THE FOUR EATON BOYS

Attend the Matinee and Avoid Waiting
Continuous from 1 P. M.
Mats., 15, 25, 35c. Eves., 25, 35, 50c.

Stanley
NO HOWARD at FRANKLIN

Her First 100% TALKING PICTURE
United Artists' Presents
MARY PICKFORD
"COQUETTE"

With Johnny Mack Brown, of Dancing Daughters
A new Mary with Boyish Bob and Flirty Eyes—"COQUETTE" is the crowning achievement of her career.

Based on the Play

National Music Week
offering
"Tannhauser" by Wagner
Mischa Guterson, Cond.

Al Wohlman on Movietone

Hit No. 1
Greater Pictures Month

PARAMOUNT FAMOUS LASKY CORP., ADOLPH ZUKOR, PRES., PARAMOUNT BLDG., N. Y.

1930

In 1930, the stage stars were taking over Hollywood. Eddie Cantor, now with the advantage of sound, became one of the most popular stars of musical films when he recreated his famous stage success *Whoopee* in technicolor. George Arliss brought two of his former stage plays to the screen, *The Green Goddess* and *Old English,* and Dennis King did a technicolor version of his stage production *The Vagabond King.* Jackie Coogan appeared in his first talking picture *Tom Sawyer,* while D. W. Griffith made one of his last films, *Abraham Lincoln,* starring Walter Huston.

America's Greatest Actor
—As You Like Him!

WARNER BROS.
present
John
BARRYMORE
in "MOBY DICK"

With JOAN BENNETT
Lloyd Hughes, and a Great Cast

FOR seven years on the seven seas he had sought the inhuman monster that had made him a man unfit to love.

Can he win revenge against this awful enemy—or will he perish in the giant maw that has been the graveyard of a hundred men before him?

Will he ever return to his home to learn that the love he thought dead is still waiting?

These are the questions that have held hundreds of thousands spellbound through the pages of Herman Melville's immortal classic, "MOBY DICK".

They are merely hints of the throbbing thrills that make "Moby Dick" John Barrymore's most glorious talking picture! See it soon, at leading theatres everywhere.

Adapted by J. Grubb Alexander. Directed by Lloyd Bacon. "Vitaphone" is the registered trademark of The Vitaphone Corporation.

A WARNER BROS. & VITAPHONE PICTURE

149

150

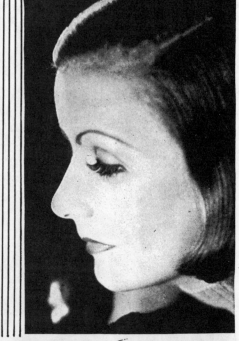

WHEN THE TEN BEST PICTURES OF 1930 ARE CHOSEN

CHARLES BICKFORD brings a vivid reality to the rugged character of the sea-hardened mate who learns the tenderness of love from Anna Christie.

GEORGE F. MARION recreates for the talking screen the hardy role of Old Mott, the unforgetably powerful characterization he made famous in the original stage production.

MARIE DRESSLER has made the world laugh with her gayety—and now she shows a new and amazing dramatic power in the role of Marthy. A portrait of the talking screen you will never forget.

CLARENCE BROWN has directed many mighty entertainments for the screen but the greatest of all is his superb picturization of O'Neill's soul stirring drama.

GRETA GARBO
IN HER FIRST ALL-TALKING PICTURE
ANNA CHRISTIE

Adapted by Frances Marion from
Eugene O'Neill's play "Anna Christie"

A CLARENCE BROWN PRODUCTION

Charles Bickford   George F. Marion   Marie Dressler

This soul-stirring drama of America's greatest playwright, Eugene O'Neill, will surely be selected for Filmdom's Hall of Fame! Gréta Garbo sounds the very depths of human emotions in her portrayal of Anna Christie, the erring woman who finally finds true love in the heart of a man big enough to forgive. A performance that places her definitely among the great actresses of all time. Don't miss this thrill!

HAROLD LLOYD

"FEET FIRST"

HAPPY days are here again! Here comes Harold with a brand new bag of tricks that will make your sides ache with laughter! Fun no end, thrills galore, action every second. ¶ Harold Lloyd's All-Talking picture "Feet First." Your eyes will be glued to the screen and you'll hang on every word! More than a motion picture—an *event* the whole family looks forward to with keen anticipation. Get set now for the great gloom destroyer of 1930! Get set and go! ¶ Your Theatre Manager will gladly tell you when "Feet First" is coming to your town. Produced by Harold Lloyd Corporation. A Paramount Release. ¶ *"If it's a Paramount Picture it's the best show in town!"*

TUNE IN! Paramount Publix Radio Hour, each Tuesday Evening, 10:15 to 11 P. M. Eastern Time, over the Columbia Broadcasting System.

Paramount Pictures

PARAMOUNT PUBLIX CORPORATION, ADOLPH ZUKOR, PRES.   PARAMOUNT BLDG., NEW YORK

ALL TALKING WHIRLWIND WESTERN!

PRINCESS
Today, ending Wed.

Buck JONES in

directed by LOUIS KING

"MEN WITHOUT LAW"

The Greatest Western Star 1st Showing

A COLUMBIA PICTURE

ZANE GREY'S

THE BORDER

LEGION"

RICHARD WITH JACK
ARLEN HOLT
FAY WRAY EUGENE PALLETTE

A Paramount Picture

Ramon Novarro in

DEVIL-MAY-CARE

He won the war single-handed, but he was shell-shocked by a kiss!

Keaton, the laugh Buster, is funnier than ever before.

BUSTER **KEATON**

in the Howitzer of Howls

Dough Boys

with CLIFF EDWARDS

154

THE SCREEN'S MOST LOVABLE BANDIT CONTINUES HIS ADVENTURES IN OLD ARIZONA IN THIS GREAT OUTDOOR MOVIETONE ROMANCE

THE ARIZONA KID *with*

WARNER BAXTER
AND MONA MARIS

Greater than "In Old Arizona" and "Romance of the Rio Grande"—two pictures that established Warner Baxter as the supreme lover in outdoor roles.

An ALFRED SANTELL production

FOX FILM CORPORATION
Harley L. Clarke
President

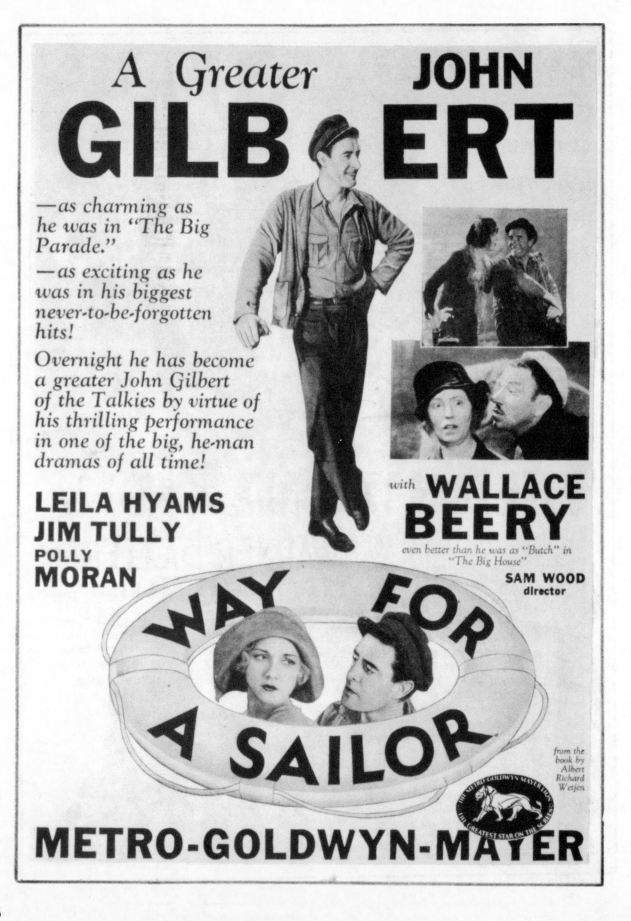

A *Greater* **JOHN GILBERT**

—as charming as he was in "The Big Parade."

—as exciting as he was in his biggest never-to-be-forgotten hits!

Overnight he has become a greater John Gilbert of the Talkies by virtue of his thrilling performance in one of the big, he-man dramas of all time!

LEILA HYAMS
JIM TULLY
POLLY MORAN

with **WALLACE BEERY**

even better than he was as "Butch" in "The Big House"

SAM WOOD director

WAY FOR A SAILOR

from the book by Albert Richard Wetjen

METRO-GOLDWYN-MAYER

TODAY:
PRICES
15c-50c

MADISON

A
PUBLIX
THEATER

Today, Monday and Tuesday

"Let's Go Native"

a
Paramount Picture

STARRING

JACK OAKIE
JEANETTE MacDONALD

With

Skeets Gallagher—Kay Francis
William Austin—Eugene Pallette

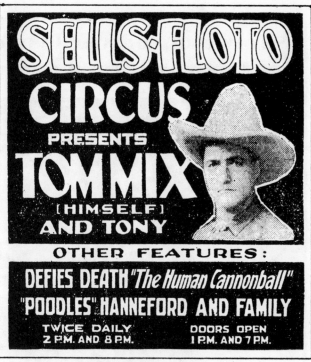

SELLS·FLOTO
CIRCUS
PRESENTS

TOM MIX
(HIMSELF)
AND TONY

OTHER FEATURES:

DEFIES DEATH "The Human Cannonball"
"POODLES" HANNEFORD AND FAMILY

TWICE DAILY
2 P.M. AND 8 P.M.

DOORS OPEN
1 P.M. AND 7 P.M.

MADISON

THE
**BENSON
MURDER
CASE**

with
William Powell

TODAY
FOR THREE DAYS
Continuous From 1 p. m.

**MURDER
IN WALL
STREET**

Was it Benson's rack-
eteer pal, or the
wealthy widow he sold
out? Was it the gorgeous
blonde he loved, or the
gigolo dancing man he
threatened? Philo Vance
leads you on a baffling
slayer hunt.

— o —

MILTON HERTH
AT THE GRAND ORGAN

ADDED

**LAUREL &
HARDY**

in

"PERFECT DAY"

—o—

Jungle Drums
Color Classic

—o—

Vitaphone Act
"What a Life"

Adm.
Child 15c
Adult 50c

"Onward, onward swords against the foe! Forward, forward the lily banners go!"

IT lives again! — the thundering throb of "Song of the Vagabonds," in the glorious golden voice of Dennis King, star of Paramount's all-color musical romance, "The Vagabond King"! Once the greatest triumph of the Broadway stage, now the supreme triumph of the talking, singing screen —Paramount's New Show World. ¶ Blazing with gorgeous Technicolor throughout . . . vibrant with stirring melodies . . . packed with thrills and adventure, excitement, romance! ¶ With Broadway's favorite romantic stars, Dennis King and Jeanette MacDonald in the leading roles, and a great cast. The New Show World of Paramount at its most brilliant height! ¶ And only Paramount, with matchless resources and unrivaled manpower, could unfold before your eyes this glittering panorama of song, color and romance in all the blazing glory of the original, the greatest of all musical romances! ¶ Don't miss the outstanding eye-and-ear treat of the year. Ask your Theatre Manager now when he is planning to show "The Vagabond King". *"If it's a Paramount Picture it's the best show in town!"*

DENNIS KING
"THE VAGABOND KING"
WITH
JEANETTE MacDONALD

Warner Oland and O. P. Heggie and cast of 1000. Ludwig Berger Production. From "If I Were King" by Justin Huntley McCarthy and "The Vagabond King" by William H. Post, Brian Hooker and Rudolph Friml.

Paramount *Pictures*

PARAMOUNT FAMOUS LASKY CORP., ADOLPH ZUKOR, PRES., PARAMOUNT BLDG., NEW YORK CITY

158

What Would You Do??

**If the man you loved wanted you to love his pal?
What did she do? What did he do? What did the
other man do?? You'll Be Surprised!**

See and Hear

THE ALL TALKING AIR SENSATION!
FLIGHT

Mighty drama of adventure in the sky with a
love theme that will grip you. Greatest and most
sensational romance and thrill triumph!

with
JACK HOLT
LILA LEE
RALPH GRAVES
and an All Star
supporting cast

A
FRANK R CAPRA
production

— Come and meet a GRAND OLD SINNER!

A "bachelor father" who
risks his name—and fortune
—for the sake of his beloved
grandchildren.

America's "First" Actor—

GEORGE
ARLISS

in Warner Bros Romantic Comedy

"Old English"

John Galsworthy's Celebrated
Play with the Child-star
of "Courage"
LEON JANNEY and
Betty Lawford, Doris Lloyd

Far more fascinating than
"Disraeli"—the most entertain-
ing role Mr. Arliss has ever had!

Publix — Balaban & Katz

ROOSEVELT
State St. near Washington St

WARNER BROS. Presents

HOLD EVERYTHING

WINNIE
LIGHTNER

JOE E.
BROWN

SALLY O'NEIL
DOROTHY REVIER
GEORGES CARPENTIER

<u>All Talking</u> Based on the
Musical Stage
Success.

ADDED VARIETIES

"EVOLUTION"
Highly amusing review of the film industry,
from penny-in-the-slot days to the all talking, color productions.

"SURPRISE"
TOM DUGAN and BARBARA LEONARD in
the most salubrious slapstick comedy since
the birth of "ye goode custard pie."

A
WARNER BROS.
& VITAPHONE
PRODUCTION

METRO
NEWS

MONDAY
and
TUESDAY

STATE
HANOVER PA.

William **HAINES**

with
ANITA PAGE
KARL DANE
J. C. NUGENT

NAVY BLUES

MADISON

A Publix Theatre
Today and Tomorrow

"Street of Chance," "Shadow of the Law" . . . and Now

WILLIAM **POWELL**

IN "For the Defense"

WITH KAY FRANCIS
a Paramount Picture

A new throbbing human drama wrested from life!

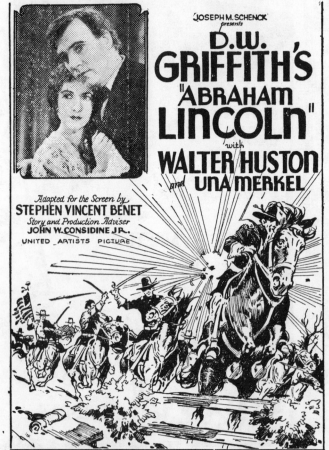

JOSEPH M. SCHENCK presents

D.W. **GRIFFITH'S** "ABRAHAM LINCOLN"

with WALTER HUSTON and UNA MERKEL

Adapted for the Screen by
STEPHEN VINCENT BENET
Story and Production Adviser
JOHN W. CONSIDINE JR.
UNITED ARTISTS PICTURE

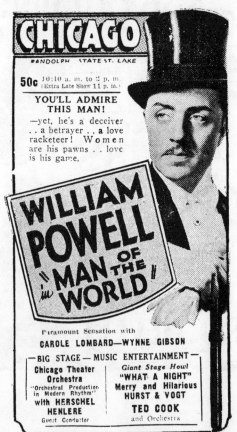

CHICAGO
RANDOLPH STATE ST. LAKE

50c 10:10 a. m. to 2 p. m.
(Extra Late Show 11 p. m.)

YOU'LL ADMIRE THIS MAN!
—yet, he's a deceiver . . a betrayer . . a love racketeer! Women are his pawns . . love is his game.

WILLIAM **POWELL** IN **MAN OF THE WORLD**

Paramount Sensation with
CAROLE LOMBARD—WYNNE GIBSON

—BIG STAGE—MUSIC ENTERTAINMENT—

Chicago Theater Orchestra
"Orchestral Production in Modern Rhythm"
WITH HERSCHEL HENLERE
Guest Conductor

Giant Stage Howl
"WHAT A NIGHT"
Merry and Hilarious
HURST & VOGT

TED COOK
and Orchestra

160

HER SIN WAS NO GREATER THAN HIS....
but SHE WAS A WOMAN

the Incomparable

NORMA SHEARER

in THE

DIVORCÉE

with

Chester Morris
Conrad Nagel
Robt. Montgomery

Directed by
Robert Z. Leonard

IF the world permits the husband to philander—why not the wife? Here is a frank, outspoken and daring drama that exposes the hypocrisy of modern marriage. Norma Shearer again proves her genius in the most dazzling performance of her career. She was wonderful in "The Last of Mrs. Cheney". She was marvelous in "Their Own Desire". She is superb in "The Divorcee" which is destined to be one of the most talked of pictures in years.

1931

By 1931, motion picture advertisements had come a long way from their crude beginning. Plain pen-and-ink drawings were replaced by sharp, well-reproduced halftone photos. The fan magazines displayed colorful, full-page announcements that were often better than the new motion pictures themselves. Gone were the electric fan cooling systems of the earlier days, for most large theaters now advertised that they were "70 degrees cool inside" and cooled by "iced air." Paramount, Pathe, Universal and Fox Movietone were now turning out weekly newsreels.

AMERICA'S MOST FASCINATING PLUNGER

SPRINGS TO VIVID LIFE ON THE SCREEN!

THE KING OF GAMBLERS
...A FOOL FOR LUCK...
A SAP FOR WOMEN

America's Most Colorful
Character ... in the Might-
iest Masterpiece of Exciting
Adventure Ever Filmed!

SMART MONEY

Warner Bros. Dynamic Smash with
EDWARD ROBINSON

In a role more romantic ...
more powerful than "Little
Caesar"..and a Brilliant Cast

Starts Tomorrow
at both Warner Theatres

CAPITOL
79th and Halsted

ORPHEUM
State and Monroe

LAST DAY
at the
CAPITOL
Richard Dix
Jackie
"Skippy"
Cooper
"DONOVAN'S KID"

WILL ROGERS
in
"A Connecticut Yankee"

As Bold Sir Boss, he is a regular Yankee Doodle at King
Arthur's Court ... wise-
cracking for all he's worth ...
the life of the party ... the
envy of the KNIGHTS ...
the despair of the flappers!

Today

Paramount

Zane Grey's
FIGHTING CARAVANS
A Paramount Picture
GARY COOPER
LILY DAMITA
ERNEST TORRENCE
TULLY MARSHALL

JAN RUBINI
with Music Masters

LLOYD HAMILTON
comedy "The Ex-
Plumber," and
Paramount News

The SPIRIT OF NOTRE DAME
with **Lew AYRES**

IS THE SPIRIT OF YOUTH

The roar of the
crowds ... bands
playing... the songs
...the cheers...the
mighty struggle ...
youth against youth
... fighting every
yard ... battling
every inch ...

Here's football ...
here's glorious
entertainment ...
drama ... love and
laughter.

with Sally Blane, William
Bakewell, J. Farrell
MacDonald, Andy De-
vine and these mighty
football heroes
CARIDEO
The Four Horsemen ...
STUHLDREHER
CROWLEY
LAYDEN
MILLER

**MULLINS, O'CONNOR,
WALSH, LAW, O'BRIEN,
McMAHON**

Directed by
RUSSELL MACK

EXTRA
Cartoon
Fly's Bride
Robt. L. Ripley
Believe It
Or Not
Stout Hearts
Frank Fay
State Theater
Sound News

More than a Gridiron Romance—a Human Triumph!

"TOUCHDOWN"

With
RICHARD ARLEN
PEGGY SHANNON
JACK OAKIE

And the finest football you've ever seen with these stars:

MORLEY DRURY
NATE BARRAGER
RUSS SAUNDERS
DALE VAN SYCKLE
HERMAN BRIX
JIM THORPE

**No Cheap Glory!
No False Heroics!**

But the most human story that was ever crowded into 70 exciting minutes!

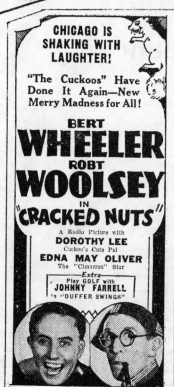

CHICAGO IS SHAKING WITH LAUGHTER!

"The Cuckoos" Have Done It Again—New Merry Madness for All!

BERT
WHEELER
ROBT
WOOLSEY
IN
"CRACKED NUTS"

A Radio Picture with
DOROTHY LEE
Cuckoo's Cute Pal
EDNA MAY OLIVER
The "Cimarron" Star

Extra
Play GOLF with
JOHNNY FARRELL
in "DUFFER SWINGS"

A New, Vital, Electrifying Beauty

MEET TALLULAH!

The picture producers who brought you Dietrich bring you another WOMAN THRILL in Donald Ogden Stewart's smashing drama.

Married to a man she doesn't love —loving a man she can't have! What does life hold for this pampered beauty of the drawing rooms?

Tarnished Lady
Starring
TALLULAH
BANKHEAD
CLIVE
BROOK

164

A Livid Face Bent Over Her In The Ghostly Mist, And

DRACULA

—her evil lover, touched her with his crimson kiss!

If you are looking for thrills—you'll find them all in this ruthless, strange, exciting drama of the "undead"!

TOD BROWNING'S Greatest Production

with

Bela Lugosi, David Manners, Helen Chandler, Dwight Frye, Edward Van Sloan, Herbert Bunston, Frances Dade, Charles Gerrard.

Loving, Riding, Fighting—He's He-Man!

TODAY! 4 DAYS

BUCK JONES in "The Fighting Sheriff"

Whirlwind Drama Spectacular Thrills

With Loretta Sayers

Directed by Louis King

A Columbia Picture

PRINCESS
COOLED BY WASHED AIR

APOLLO

Sunday, Evenings 10c-25c. Weekday Mat., 10c-15c. 1 'Till Close. Dial 4-4901

EDW. G.

TODAY ONLY ROBINSON in "TIGER SHARK"

With RICHARD ARLEN ZITA JOHANN

Tomorrow

GEORGE RAFT in "Under Cover Man" with Nancy Carroll

THEY'RE OFF!

WARNER BROS. present

AL JOLSON in "BIG BOY"

You can't clock the laughs in this entertainment classic! Take a tip! Set your bets on "Big Boy" for a killing in the entertainment sweepstakes — You'll cheer, laugh and howl as you follow Jolson as the wisecracking blackface jockey!

Big Boy Is A Big Joy!

WARNER BROS. & VITAPHONE Talking Pictures

FOX
25 Till 2 35 2 to 6 50 Nights

THE SKY'S THE LIMIT WHEN PAPA STEPS OUT!

Will himself . . . All dolled up and plenty of places to go . . . With a naughty French gal to keep things humming . . .

WILL ROGERS

In His Latest and Best Cure for the Blues

YOUNG AS YOU FEEL

with FIFI DORSAY

LUCIEN LITTLEFIELD

CLIVE BROOK   FAY WRAY   RICHARD ARLEN   JEAN ARTHUR   BUDDY ROGERS

THESE FIVE PARAMOUNT STARS

Offer a Performance Seldom Equaled on the Talking Screen!

"THE LAWYER'S SECRET"

EXTRA! All 3 Theaters
See Post-Gatty—World Flyers!
Triumphant Return in
Paramount Sound News

Two Women in Love! One Ready to Sacrifice Her All for Her Man—the Other Willing to Sacrifice Her Sweetheart for Her Family's Reputation!

ANOTHER GREAT ROLE—ANOTHER BLAZING TRIUMPH FOR THE WINNER OF THE 1930 BEST PERFORMANCE AWARD

NORMA SHEARER

in

STRANGERS MAY KISS

This is the statue awarded to Norma Shearer by the Academy of Motion Picture Arts and Sciences, for her performance in "The Divorcee," the best given by any actress during 1930.

To him it was just another episode—to her, a dream she could never forget.

SHE faced life fearlessly — accepted love where she found it—because she believed a woman could "kiss and forget" even as a man does. But heartbreak and cruel disillusionment lay between her and ultimate happiness with the one man in all the world whom she did love.... If you enjoyed Norma Shearer in "The Divorcee"—don't miss her in this dramatic picture based on Ursula Parrott's sensational novel.

with ROBERT MONTGOMERY
NEIL HAMILTON   MARJORIE RAMBEAU
and IRENE RICH
Directed by
GEORGE FITZMAURICE

Robert Montgomery who helped Norma Shearer make her great success in "The Divorcee" is again seen with her.

Ursula Parrott, author of "The Divorcee" has written another absorbing story. Don't miss it!

THE METRO-GOLDWYN-MAYER LION
THE GREATEST STAR ON THE SCREEN

EXTRA! M-G-M NEWS EXTRA!

THE KNOCKOUT PICTURE OF THE YEAR!

Don't fail to get a ringside seat at your favorite movie theatre to see Wallace Beery as "the Champ" fight for his boy, Dink (Jackie Cooper). You will be thrilled beyond words by this story of a battered, broken down pugilist trying to stage a comeback because his boy believes him to be the greatest fighter in the world. You will not be ashamed to brush away a tear as the Champ makes his last great sacrifice for his boy. And you will say, with millions of other movie fans, "Beery is great — Jackie Cooper is marvelous — The Champ is truly the knockout picture of the year!"

He loved this boy of his more than anything else in the world—but knew that the best thing he could do for him was to go out of his life forever . . . a world of pathos and cheer in a picture you will never forget!

WALLACE · JACKIE
BEERY · COOPER
The CHAMP

with Irene RICH — Roscoe ATES

A KING VIDOR PRODUCTION

Story by Frances Marion   Dialogue Continuity by Leonard Praskins

A METRO - GOLDWYN - MAYER *Picture*

PRINCESS
Today and Tomorrow
The Black Shadow rides again!
BUCK JONES in The Avenger
A COLUMBIA PICTURE

all action WESTERN!
BUCK JONES in "The TEXAS RANGER"

ALL CHICAGO HAILS
THIS 1931 ROMANCE!
Doug Reaches the Peak of His
Career in This Modern Role!
DOUGLAS
FAIRBANKS
"REACHING FOR THE MOON"
with BEBE DANIELS

RICHARD
DIX
JACKIE
COOPER
Sensational Star of
SKIPPY
YOUNG
DONOVAN'S
KID

Crashes Society in Swiped Suit
Youth's Nerve Wins Millionaire's Support!
Wm. HAINES
in M-G-M's riotous comedy from the stage hit
A Tailor Made Man
With
Dorothy Gordon   Joseph Cawthorn
Marjorie Rambeau   William Austin
A PUBLIX THEATRE
MADISON
THEATRE
Continuous, 1 Till Closing

The Flaming
Empress
of "IT"
PARKWAY
NORTH AVE. at CHARLES ST.
CLARA BOW in
'Love Among
the Millionaires"
A Paramount Picture   Comedy! Revue! News!

170

EXCLUSIVE SHOWING IN CENTRAL ILLINOIS—HIS NEW $2,000,000 PICT!
PRICES TODAY—ADULTS, 50c; CHILDREN, 25c. SHOWS AT 10:00, 11:45 A. M.; 1:30, 3:15, 5

Charlie Chaplin

CITY LIGHTS

The old favorite, better known than the ABC's, is back in a pulsating story of how the other half and our own half lives . . . From city tramp, he turns to an Alexander and looks for other worlds to conquer as a white wing, leather pusher, yea, even a jail bird.

SPECIAL NOTICE!
Owing to the nature of the contract made for this picture there will be no Special Ladies' Guest Matinees at the Princess and no Bargain Nights at the Columbia during run of this picture. NO FREE LIST.

WRITTEN, DIRECTED AND PRODUCED by CHARLES CHAPLIN

UNITED ARTISTS PICTURE

Laughs catch up the sobs -- the fun is fast and furious and that forlorn figure with the battered derby and the baggy trousers comes through the laugh knockout of the century!

A Riot of Mirth!

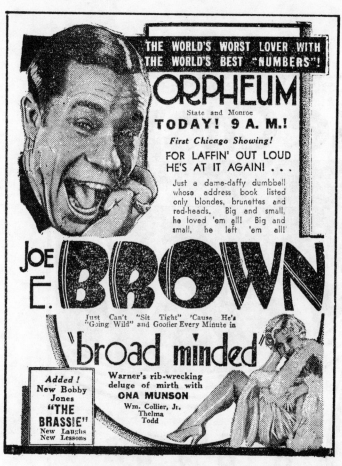

THE WORLD'S WORST LOVER WITH THE WORLD'S BEST "NUMBERS"!

ORPHEUM

State and Monroe

TODAY! 9 A. M.!

First Chicago Showing!

FOR LAFFIN' OUT LOUD HE'S AT IT AGAIN! . . .

Just a dame-daffy dumbbell whose address book listed only blondes, brunettes and red-heads. Big and small, he loved 'em all! Big and small, he left 'em all!

JOE E. BROWN

Just Can't "Sit Tight" 'Cause He's "Going Wild" and Goofier Every Minute in

"broad minded"

Warner's rib-wrecking deluge of mirth with

ONA MUNSON

Wm. Collier, Jr.
Thelma Todd

Added! New Bobby Jones "THE BRASSIE" New Laughs New Lessons

ZANE GREY'S

RIDERS of the PURPLE SAGE

Fox Picture with
GEORGE O'BRIEN

Marguerite Churchill
Noah Beery

VENGEANCE SPURRED HIM ON—UNTIL LOVE LASSOED HIM! Hair trigger action in a smashing romance of the Southwest.

ROOSEVELT

STATE ST. near WASHINGTON

35c—9 A. M. to 1—50c—1 to 6 P. M.

TODAY—Drama Unleashing a Thousand Wild Passions . . . Ablaze with Exultant Love . . . Afire with Fierce Hate!

JOHN BARRYMORE

in

"The MAD GENIUS"

Warner Bros.' Triumph, With

MARION MARSH   DONALD COOK
   CARMEL MYERS
Charles Butterworth—Luis Alberni

He Was Mad — Yet His Madness Was to Pour His Soul Into Others — to Bring Them the Fame That Was His Birthright!

ADULTS ONLY
CENSORS' ORDERS

172

"MOROCCO," "THE BLUE ANGEL"—*never before has anyone leaped into such instant popularity as glorious, glamorous Marlene Dietrich, "with the wisdom of the ages in her eyes."*

VICTOR McLAGLEN
MARLENE DIETRICH
in
"*Dishonored*"

Story and direction by JOSEF VON STERNBERG

To tell you the story would spoil it. It must be seen. So true to her part is Marlene Dietrich you live every minute of the picture. Vibrant, alive, telling—right to the end she carries you. And you go out of the theatre with the deep satisfaction that comes with leaving for a while your own life and experiencing the life of another. ¶ A typical Paramount production, which means—the cast is flawless, the story absorbing, the "atmosphere" authentic—unmistakably *A Paramount Picture* and "*the best show in town!*"

Paramount 🔺 *Pictures*

Paramount Publix Corp., Adolph Zukor, Pres., Paramount Bldg., N.Y

RKO STATE·LAKE
OPEN 10:30 AM 50¢ to 2 P.M.

"CIM"
ROARS
INTO
CHI!

EDNA FERBER
America's foremost
Author Wrote Her
Heart Out Telling
This Immortal Love
Story—and

THE SCREEN
KEEPS FAITH!

TALKIES
REBORN IN
GLORIOUS
PAGEANT!
STANDS BIG
TOWN ON
ITS HEAD!
PRESS SHRIEKS
ACCLAMATION!

with
RICHARD DIX
Irene Dunne
Estelle Taylor
and a cast of
10,000

CIMARRON

Radio Pictures

LOVE WAS THE
WINNING
CARD—

...in a hand dealt by
death!
A knave demanded
his life—but a queen
saved it!

RKO PATHE presents
BILL BOYD
THE
BIG GAMBLE

DOROTHY SEBASTIAN · WARNER
OLAND · JAMES GLEASON

A Charles R. Rogers Production
Harry Joe Brown, Asso. Producer

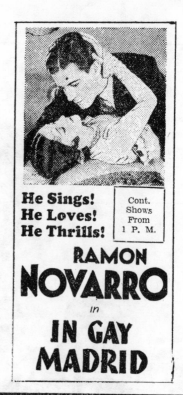

He Sings!
He Loves!
He Thrills!

Cont.
Shows
From
1 P. M.

RAMON
NOVARRO
in
**IN GAY
MADRID**

ORIENTAL
RANDOLPH near STATE
10:45 A. M. to 1 P. M., 35c

LADIES and GENTLEMEN
Come! See Whoopee Bill
Go Western in a rodeo
of roars, romance and
red-blooded action!

WM. HAINES
POLLY MORAN
and Leila Hyams in
"WAY OUT WEST"
A Metro Romance with
CLIFF EDWARDS
Full of gals—guns and gags!

What a Stage Show!
HARRY
ROSE
in "Bohemian Nights"
With
World Champion
Marathon Dancers
ANN GERRY
MIKE GOUVAS
In Person!

PALACE
TODAY
and Tomorrow
Prices Today: 10c-40c

Child 10c
Adult 40c

He thinks it is a
MAN'S WAR—until
he meets the Sweet-
heart of the Army!

**GARY
COOPER**
in
"A
**Man from
Wyoming**"
a Paramount Picture

Big boss of the front-
lines—he meets a fighter
who won't be bossed—
and marries her!
Then what? June
Collyer with the
star of "The Vir-
ginian!"

EXTRA ADDED FEATURE
**LAUREL
& HARDY**
In Latest Comedy Scream
"COME CLEAN"

BEBE DANIELS

"Vitaphone" is the registered trademark of The Vitaphone Corporation.

"My Past"

The tell-tale autobiography of DORA MACY'S life!

BEN LYON
LEWIS STONE
JOAN BLONDELL
NATALIE MOORHEAD
Screen adaptation and dialogue
by Charles Kenyon
Directed by ROY DEL RUTH

Beautiful, alluring — surrounded by men, yet always lonely; showered by luxuries, yet unhappy — love and marriage offered her, but always the dark shadow of her past to come between her and happiness! Dora Macy, the girl whose missteps forever echoed to haunt her! You have read her famous story which the authoress dared not sign. Now see it brought to life with the glamorous Bebe Daniels, playing the part of a modern girl whom men remembered — but women can never forget!

A WARNER BROS. & VITAPHONE PICTURE

175

1932

The country was now deep in the depression. With widespread unemployment, movie attendance dwindled. In an effort to bolster sagging receipts, theater managers introduced "two-for one" passes, "bank night," "dish night," "bingo" and "double features." Admission prices at some of the "first-run houses" were reduced to as low as 20¢ for matinees and 30¢ for evening shows. Among the newcomers to the screen were Johnny Weissmuller in his first Tarzan picture, Katherine Hepburn and George Raft. Laurel & Hardy appeared in their second feature-length comedy, *Pack Up Your Troubles*. At Universal Pictures, Tom Mix made his first talking western, *Destry Rides Again*.

TWO ADVENTURERS OF FORTUNE

They lived and fought for thrills and love

WAR CORRESPONDENT

with

Jack HOLT   Ralph GRAVES

LILA LEE

Directed by Paul Sloane

FINAL SHOWINGS
Chained to the Mob

...While the world cried "peekaboo!"

Constance BENNETT

pays for fame in

"WHAT PRICE HOLLYWOOD"

with LOWELL SHERMAN
GREGORY RATOFF
NEIL HAMILTON
Directed by George Cukor.

ALSO
Last of the Mohicans
Chapter 3
Robert L. Ripley,
Believe It Or Not

PRINCESS
TODAY!
and Tomorrow

You've Never Seen Such Thrill-Speed!

Buck JONES in *High Speed*

with
Loretta Sayers
Directed by
D. Ross Lederman
A Columbia
Picture

Tense Drama of the Speedway!

"One Way Passage"

WILLIAM POWELL   KAY FRANCIS

"By all means don't miss 'One Way Passage.' It's one of the best."
—CAOL FRINK, Examiner.

"Repays your outlay at the box office with a real hour of enjoyment."
—MAE TINEE, Tribune.

JOAN
CRAWFORD
(Courtesy
Metro-Goldwyn-Mayer)
in
RAIN
with WALTER HUSTON

**NO ADVANCE
IN PRICES**

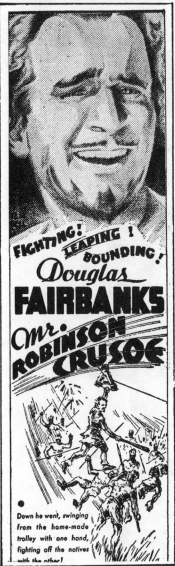

FIGHTING!
LEAPING!
BOUNDING!
**Douglas
FAIRBANKS**
Mr.
**ROBINSON
CRUSOE**

Down he went, swinging
from the home-made
trolley with one hand,
fighting off the natives
with the other!

FIRST TIME AT POPULAR PRICES

TODAY . . . for a Full Week —**HERE AT LAST**—
The Most Startling Drama Ever Produced!

Dazzling Norma Shearer, the soul of all women, trapped
in a tangled love-life—passionately adored by Clark Gable,
greatest of all screen lovers. *What a combination!*

★★★ **her three men**

loving them all . . clinging to each for what
he makes of her . . a woman suspected . .
a woman desired . . a woman possessed!

Norma **SHEARER**
Clark **GABLE**
in MGM'S *daringly real picture*
'Strange Interlude'

Alexander Kirkland • Maureen O'Sullivan
Ralph Morgan • May Robson • Robert Young

. ALSO .

ARTHUR TRACY, "Street Singer,"
in "REACHING FOR THE MOON"

Paramount Sound News Events

IMPORTANT!
SEE IT
FROM THE
BEGINNING
Feature Starts:
1:00, 3:05, 5:15
7:20, 9:30

Publix . . .

■ 10c - 40c ■   **MADISON**

CONTINUOUS, ONE TILL CLOSE—DIAL 4-4901

179

Sure it's their NEW FULL - LENGTH FUN FILM and every inch is a HOWL!

After the success of this happy pair of comedians in their first feature-length comedy·"Pardon Us" audiences demanded another. Here it is—6 reels full of bubbling, boisterous laughs. See it and *you'll* "pack up your troubles"! Hooray for Laurel and Hardy!

STAN
LAUREL

OLIVER
HARDY

Let's all thank HAL ROACH for his Mint of Merriment!

WAR! WAR!

PACK UP YOUR TROUBLES

180

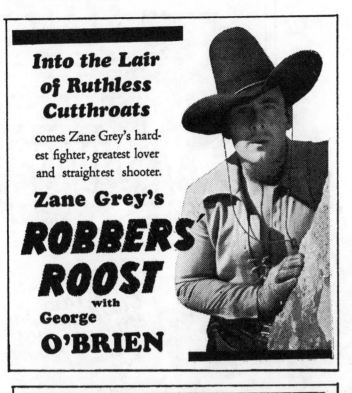

Into the Lair of Ruthless Cutthroats

comes Zane Grey's hardest fighter, greatest lover and straightest shooter.

Zane Grey's

ROBBERS' ROOST

with George

O'BRIEN

FACING A FLAMING DEATH,...FOR FIFTY DOLLARS! Real war heroes fight the gory BATTLE OF HOLLYWOOD

in

THE LOST SQUADRON

ONCE he risked his life for his country... now he takes the same deadly chances to give you a moment's thrill!

Shot at only by cameras... yet falling in flames! Ordered to die by a jealous movie director—before the horrified eyes of the girl he loves!

Diving, looping, crashing through this RKO drama from the Liberty magazine serial,
starring

RICHARD DIX

with

MARY ASTOR   JOEL McCREA
ERICH von STROHEIM
DOROTHY JORDAN
and a cast of famous flyers

A PUBLIX THEATRE

MADISON THEATRE

Dial 4-4901   Continuous 1 till Clos'ng
Sunday (all day) 15c-50c
Weekday Mat. 10c-40c   Eve. 15c-50c

—ALSO—

FORD STERLING
in a comedy howl
"TWENTY HORSES"

LONDON—a city of Tradition

Paramount Sound News Events

THE LEGION OF THE DAMNED!

Hells Island, surrounded by sharks, guarded by guns—a seething cauldron of hating men—murder lurks in every corner—"The Legion of the Damned" are they—Desperate men—cunning, cruel, scheming!

ALL-TALKING!   !ALL-THRILLS!   ALL-ACTION

TWO MEN
AND A GIRL!

—And what a girl! She was true to the entire Foreign Legion! Love 'em and leave 'em was her motto! She was the most famous dancer of Bel-Abbas—a—nd when she danced—oh, baby!

If you liked "Flight" and "Submarinee"—

DON'T MISS—

"HELL'S ISLAND"

with

JACK HOLT
RALPH GRAVES
DOROTHY SEBASTIAN

— Also —
JOE FRISCO
in the All
Talking
Comedy Act
"MY SUGAR"

At The Height Of Her Glory!

Greta

GARBO

as you Desire Me

A Metro-Goldwyn-Mayer PICTURE

COOL & COMFORTABLE

CAPITOL

MORRISON and 4th Avenue

READ BY MILLIONS
NOW a Motion Picture
"The Night Club Lady" with
ADOLPHE MENJOU
Mayo Methot · Skeets Gallagher

ENJOY A GOOD SHOW IN THE COOL STATE

STATE LAST TIMES TODAY

What a riot when this monarch of muscle men turns from hi-jacking to high-life — from homicide to house parties—from dames to debutantes!

Extra
Cartoon
Ocean Hop
State
News

EDWARD G. ROBINSON

FIRST NATIONAL HIT

LITTLE GIANT

MARY ASTOR
HELEN VINSON

Love Rides the Clouds at 200 Miles an Hour!

Cloud-Bursting, Heart-Bursting Daredevils...Risking Their Necks for the Love of a Beautiful Girl!

Thrills follow thrills, in

"SKY BRIDE"

WITH

RICHARD ARLEN
JACK OAKIE
ROBERT COOGAN

A Paramount Picture

—Also—
COMEDY—NOVELTY—NEWS.

TODAY! FOR TWO DAYS ONLY
A Publix Theatre

MADISON THEATRE

Continuous 1 till Closing. Dial 4-4961. Sunday (all day) 15c-50c. Weekday Mats. 10c-40c. Weekday Eves. 15c-50c.

COMING TUESDAY
The Miracle Picture
"The Miracle Man"

STRANGE DESIRES

...loves and hates and secret yearnings... hidden in the shadows of a man's mind.

DR·JEKYLL AND MR·HYDE

a Paramount Picture

Fredric MARCH in His Most Distinctive Role!

Miriam HOPKINS Tempestuous....Utterly Fascinating!

TODAY! FOR FOUR BIG DAYS.....

"THE CHAMP" in a heart warming role! Strength of a giant . . . trusting heart of a child . . . he sacrificed his career for the smile of a woman's lying lips!

WALLACE BEERY in "Flesh"

—WITH—

KAREN MORLEY   **RICARDO CORTEZ**
JEAN HERSHOLT   JOHN MILGAN

ALSO
"Santa's Work Shop" Silly Symphony

"Duck Huater's Paradise"—Novelty

Paramount News

10c 40c   **PUBLIX MADISON**   10c 40c

CONTINUOUS, 1 'TILL CLOSE—DIAL 4-4901

184

FEARLESS LOVERS....
courageously they faced life's hardships
...boldly they carved an empire!!!......

RICHARD **DIX**
ANN **HARDING**
The **CONQUERORS**

TODAY! FOR
3 MIGHTY DAYS!

A tidal drama of America——deep as human passion
With **EDNA MAY OLIVER** · **GUY**
KIBBEE *Julie Haydon* "Skeets" *Gallagher*

—— ALSO ——
"THE DENTIST," Comedy Howl
Hawaian Fantasy, Novelty
Paramount News in Sound

PUBLIX **MADISON**

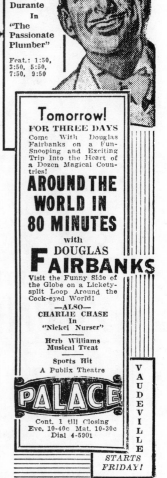

LAST TIMES
TODAY!
Buster
Keaton
Polly
Moran
Jimmy
Durante
In
"The
Passionate
Plumber"

Feat.: 1:50,
3:50, 5:50,
7:50, 9:50

Tomorrow!
FOR THREE DAYS
Come With Douglas
Fairbanks on a Fun-
Snooping and Exciting
Trip Into the Heart of
a Dozen Magical Coun-
tries!

**AROUND THE
WORLD IN
80 MINUTES**

with
DOUGLAS
FAIRBANKS

Visit the Funny Side of
the Globe on a Lickety-
split Loop Around the
Cock-eyed World!

——ALSO——
CHARLIE CHASE
In
"Nickel Nurser"

Herb Williams
Musical Treat

Sports Hit

A Publix Theatre

PALACE

Cont. 1 till Closing
Eve. 10-40c Mat. 10-30c
Dial 4-5901

VAUDEVILLE

STARTS
FRIDAY!

TODAY
FOR 3
DAYS
A NEW
FU MANCHU
THRILLER!

SIREN OF SHANGHAI
Even she . . . the cruelest
beauty of the East learns
the pang of a lovelorn heart
**"THE MASK OF
FU MANCHU"**

They danced with death when they lingered in her secret
garden . . . for behind this golden lily of the Orient
. . . was Dr Fu Manchu . . . using her unearthly beauty
to draw unsuspecting men into the toils of his incredible
revenge.

with **BORIS KARLOFF**
LEWIS STONE — KAREN MORLEY — MYRNA LOY
CHAS. STARRETT — JEAN HERSHOLT

ALSO :. "TORCHY ROLLS HIS OWN"—Comedy
MOVIETONE NEWS EVENTS

10c
30c
Publix **PALACE**
10c
30c

Continuous One 'Till Closing.   Dial 4-5901

185

Edw. G. Robinson

THE SCREEN'S GREATEST CHARACTER ACTOR

in

"The HATCHET MAN"

with LORETTA YOUNG

as Toya San the beautiful butterfly broken on the wheel of life.

DUDLEY DIGGES

Based on a play by Achmed Abdullah and David Belasco . . . Screen play by J. Grubb Alexander . . . Directed by

WILLIAM A. WELLMAN

Purple nights! . . . Words of love! . . . All the witchery of the mystic East with its tangled skeins of human passion pervades "The Hatchet Man" . . . It is a symphony of blazing emotions . . . Stark, elemental drama—of a man who gives—of a woman who takes—of a butterfly who singes her wings at forbidden flames . . . Thrilling! powerful! breath-taking! with the screen's most versatile character actor scaling the highest peak of emotional portrayal.

A FIRST NATIONAL & VITAPHONE PICTURE

JOE E. **BROWN** in The **TENDERFOOT**

with GINGER ROGERS and LEW CODY

A Bronco Buster Who Went Busted on Broadway

TOGETHER!

THEY WERE BORN TO LOVE! . . . .

The Flaming Lovers of the Screen, in a Tempestuous Drama of Primitive Passions and Adventure!

CLARK **GABLE** Jean **HARLOW**

Red Dust

Special Comedy Attraction **LAUREL** and **HARDY** in "ANY OLD PORT"

A How!—a Laugh—a Scream Every Second with the Kings of Mirth!

ENDS TODAY "It's Great to Be Alive," with Edna May Oliver

TOMORROW! WHERE LIFE IS ACTION! Zane Grey's **LIFE IN THE RAW** with George O'Brien

—ALSO— MICKEY McGUIRE in "Mickey's Big Broadcast"

*   *   *

CARTOON   NEWS

PALACE

20c Till 6; After, 30c; Child 10; Dial 4-5901

187

JOHN BARRYMORE

Pours his burning soul into one of the finest living documents the stage has ever given to the screen . . . Clemence Dane's magnificent play . . .

A BILL OF DIVORCEMENT

With
KATHARINE HEPBURN
Billie Burke, David Manners

Trapped like rats in the path of Tartar bandit hordes in war-torn Manchuria!

RICHARD DIX

With the Year's Most Beautiful Screen Find

Gwili Andre
Popular Nordic Beauty

EDWARD E. HORTON
ARLINE   JUDGE
ZASU   PITTS
DUDLEY   DIGGES

Strident! Heroic! In drama ripped from the news of today!

ROAR OF THE DRAGON

STARTS TODAY!
COLONIAL

ALSO
TOM HOWARD COMEDY
→ CURIOSITIES
→ NEWS

Lean Back and Laugh!

The First Harold Lloyd Comedy, and His Funniest in Two Years Is Here Today—for Five Big Days!

A 1932-33 Laugh Triumph!

HAROLD LLOYD
in
"Movie Crazy"

Paramount's New Season Smash With
CONSTANCE CUMMINGS

It's New . . . It's Unusual . . . It's Original!

Also   Betty Boop for President
Fighting Fins
Paramount News

PUBLIX MADISON

Continuous, 1 till Closing
10c-40c (No Tax)   Dial 4-4901

1933

Will Rogers was now one of the most popular stars in Hollywood and Joe E. Brown was one of the most hilarious of the new talking picture comedians. Bing Crosby was just starting his long career at Paramount Pictures in *College Humor* and *Too Much Harmony*. Fred Astaire appeared in his first picture in a small part as Joan Crawford's dancing partner in *Dancing Lady*. John Barrymore was in constant demand, dividing his time making films for R.K.O., Universal, and Metro-Goldwyn-Mayer all in one year. Marie Dressler and Wallace Beery made their second picture together, *Tugboat Annie*.

FILM'S GREATEST TEAM IN A MUSICAL ROMANCE! **TODAY**

Joan **CRAWFORD**
Clark **GABLE** *in*
Dancing Lady

With FRANCHOT TONE—MAY ROBSON
WINNIE LIGHTNER—FRED ASTAIRE
TED HEALY AND HIS STOOGES

15¢ Till 2 (Sun.)
Till 6 On
Week Days
Dial 4-4901

APOLLO

25¢ After 2 (Sun.)
After 6 Week
Days
Child 10c

Great States

COOL
Palace
1 TILL CLOSE—DIAL 4-5901

20c Till 5 P. M.; Till 6 P. M. Weekdays
After 6 P. M. 30c; Children 10c

TODAY! FOR 3 DAYS!
1933's Greatest Drama of Humanity!

An inspiring drama of today, that
will move you to cheers and tears
...with Barrymore living
a role you'll never forget!

Lionel
BARRYMORE
Thrills Your Soul in

LOOKING FORWARD

with
LEWIS STONE   BENITA HUME

—ALSO—

OUR GANG in
"Fish Hookey"
● CARTOON
SOUND NEWS

EDDIE CANTOR *in*

"ROMAN SCANDALS"

Your Eddie! Our Eddie! Everybody's Eddie! Now a crashing
charioteer! Burning up Rome with
laughs, lions, lovely ladies, lilting
lyrics! One big Roman Holiday!

with RUTH ETTING
GLORIA STUART
DAVID MANNERS
and the
NEW GOLDWYN GIRLS

UNITED ARTISTS

Starts Tomorrow!

LAUGHING–LOVING–FIGHTING HELL-HOUNDS OF THE SEA!

Flirting with love, then with death . . . out of the warm arms of women . . . into the cold grip of the sea. Reckless Don Juans ashore—men of iron afloat!

ROMANCE, COMEDY AND SPECTACLE NEVER BEFORE PRESENTED ON THE SCREEN

HELL BELOW

ROBERT MONTGOMERY

MADGE EVANS
JIMMY DURANTE
ROBERT YOUNG
EUGENE PALLETTE
WALTER HUSTON

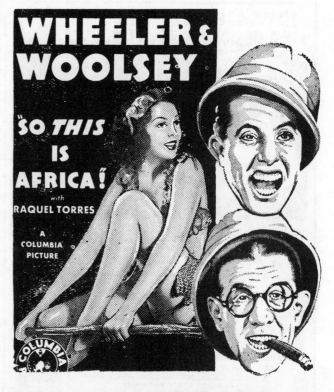

WHEELER & WOOLSEY

"SO THIS IS AFRICA!"

with RAQUEL TORRES

A COLUMBIA PICTURE

10c 30c

PALACE

Cont. 1 Till Close   Dial 4-5901

TODAY! FOR 3 THRILLING DAYS!

IT COMES TO LIFE!

BURIED ALIVE---
A Love 3000 Years Old Brings It Back!

The Master of Makeup In His Most Amazing Story.

KARLOFF

THE UNCANNY . . . IN

THE MUMMY

with

ZITA JOHANN
ARTHUR BYRON
DAVID MANNERS

ALSO
JOE PENNER in "Here Prince"
Cartoon Song
Movietone News

This picture is highly recommended and endorsed by the Rosicrucian Order (AMORC), which recommends that all members in this community attend this unusual picture.

93 FEATURED PLAYERS!

STARTING TODAY!

OUT OF A great picture rises a new star . . . watch her face . . . her grace . . . her passion! She doesn't make love . . . she lives it!

ONLY YESTERDAY . . . .
she was happy in the arms of the only man she could ever love!

ONLY YESTERDAY . . . .
and then thousands of empty "to-days" . . . Here is the heart-cry of the woman forsaken! . . . Here at last is full mission, of the talking screen!

ADDED FUN CHARLEY CHASE Comedy Riot

ONLY YESTERDAY

By the Director of "BACK STREET"

MARGARET SULLAVAN
JOHN BOLES

Edna May Oliver   Reginald Denny
Billie Burke   Onslow Stevens
Jimmie Butler   Benita Hume

25c Till 7   35c Nights

ORIENTAL
JOHN HAMRICK'S
GRAND AVE at E. MORRISON

8 STARS IN ONE PICTURE

The season's greatest cast in a story that pulses with the romance, excitement and gayety of a big State Fair . . . A love idyll between a country lass and a reporter . . . Father and Mother busy winning prizes . . . Son finding adventure with a carnival girl who loved him but left him.

FOX FILM presents

Janet GAYNOR   Will ROGERS
Lew AYRES   Sally EILERS
Norman Foster   Louise Dresser
Frank Craven   Victor Jory

STATE FAIR

From the story by PHIL STONG
Screen play by SONYA LEVIEN and PAUL GREEN

HENRY KING PRODUCTION

An Outstanding All-Star Screen Smash!

CLARK GABLE
HELEN HAYES
JOHN BARRYMORE
ROB'T. MONTGOMERY
LIONEL BARRYMORE
MYRNA LOY

"NIGHT FLIGHT"

a METRO picture

LAST TIMES TODAY! Doors open 9:30
SALLY RAND   "Penthouse"
PAT ROONEY   WARNER BAXTER
SEAMAN BROTHERS   Myrna Loy • Mae Clarke
RAYMOND BAIRD

COLONIAL

◆◆◆ RICHARD
DIX
in
THE
GREAT JASPER

The private
life of a
free-lance
lover.

with
WERA ENGELS
EDNA MAY OLIVER
Bruce Cabot, Florence
Eldridge, Betty Furness

Directed by
J. Walter Ruben
David O. Selznick

TODAY!---FOR 3 DAYS

Blondes..Brunettes..and Their Bank Rolls!
'He Makes 'Em! . . . Takes 'Em and Tosses 'Em
Away! Wild Jimmy in a Knockout Riot of Laughs!

JAMES CAGNEY

IN

"JIMMY the GENT"

with

BETTE DAVIS
Alice White

ALSO: TOM HOWARD in "DIVORCE SWEETS"
Norman Terris in "Around the Clock"   News Events

PALACE

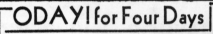

● TODAY! for Four Days

"If Wives Only
Knew What We
Know - About
Their Husbands"

He Was a Flirt!
His Wife Knew
It! But she never
knew Why until
she met his beau-
tiful young
sweetheart!

Ann Robert
HARDING MONTGOMERY

In Rachel Crother's Daring
Broadway Hit—now a
screen sensation!

When Ladies Meet

WITH
**MYRNA
LOY
ALICE BRADY
FRANK MORGAN**

ALSO
THELMA TODD and
ZASU PITTS
in "Bargain of the Century"
MUSICAL   NEWS

MADISON

MADISON

30c Till 6, After 40c
Child 10c
1 Till Close   Dial 4-4901

TODAY and
TOMORROW!

Ninety
Minutes
of Fun!

The Kings of
Comedy run-
ning riot
through the
World's Fair.

A
Howl!

Stan **LAUREL**
Oliver **HARDY**

in their great-
est full length
feature.

Sons OF THE DESERT

with **CHARLEY
CHASE**

—EXTRA—
ETHEL WATERS in "Rufus Jones
for President" most sensational
short ever made.
BABY ROSE MARIE in
"Sing Babies, Sing"
Paramount News

NOW PLAYING!

THEY LEAP FROM THE BOOK AND *LIVE!* ...

The world's most beloved family of girls... in the picture America has waited three quarters of a century to see!

The electric lady of "Morning Glory" brings to the screen a new sensation of loveliness!

Katharine **HEPBURN**

in "Little Women"

by LOUISA MAY ALCOTT

with

JOAN BENNETT
PAUL LUKAS
FRANCES DEE
JEAN PARKER
Edna May Oliver
Douglass Montgomery
Henry Stephenson

HOLIDAYS—
25c Till 5 P. M. **35**c Nights
Children 10¢ Anytime

EXTRA EARLY SHOW! 9:00 A. M. SATURDAY
Come Early and Avoid the Crowds!

JOHN HAMRICK'S Music Box

UNITED ARTISTS: *Wednesday*

"I'VE SEEN sharks getting men at sea! Women getting men on land! Fatheads getting tight! Redheads getting loose! Hell popping and nobody stopping... at anything... to 'get' their woman.... and 'get' their man!"

I COVER THE WATERFRONT

CLAUDETTE **COLBERT**
BEN LYON

ENDS TUESDAY ... MARY PICKFORD IN "SECRETS"

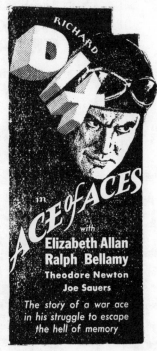

RICHARD **DIX**

in *ACE of ACES*

with

Elizabeth Allan
Ralph Bellamy

Theodore Newton
Joe Sauers

The story of a war ace in his struggle to escape the hell of memory

---

TOMORROW NITE
Big Midnight Show 11:45
All Seats 40c
Reserved None

"TOO MUCH HARMONY"

A Paramount Picture with ..

BING CROSBY
and JACK OAKIE
SKEETS GALLAGHER
Judith Allen   Harry Green
Lilyan Tashman   Ned Sparks

MADISON

THEY MIGHT BE THE FAMILY NEXT DOOR!
...But If They Were You'd Move!!!

Meet the Rimplegars...Just One
Big Sappy Family..Part Squirrely
and 100% Nuts..Yet Gosh-Awful
Human Endearing Folks!

Tomorrow
Look What a Cast..
Claudette
COLBERT
Richard
ARLEN
Mary
BOLAND

Tom Brown,
Lyda Roberti,
Wallace Ford,
Joan Marsh,
Hardie Albright,
Wm. Bakewell

IN

"THREE CORNERED MOON"

TODAY

An EXPLOSION of LAUGHS!

—PLUS—
VAUDE-
VILLE
and
STAGE
BAND

Jean HARLOW IN
"BLONDE BOMBSHELL"
LEE TRACY

ARE YOU
THIRSTY?
for laughs?

Then see what
Buster and
"Schnozzle"
have brewed
for your de-
light!

Buster
KEATON
Jimmy
DURANTE

Follow
the crowds
and laugh,
laugh, laugh.

WHAT!
NO BEER?

with
ROSCOE ATES, PHYLLIS
BARRY, JOHN MILJAN

A Metro Goldwyn Mayer PICTURE

● HE'S HERE TODAY! FOR A BIG
WEEK...IN HIS
GREATEST HIT
America's Best Loved
Star in America's Most
Beloved Story

WILL
ROGERS
in Fox Film's grand and glorious
"DAVID HARUM"
with
EVELYN VENABLE
LOUISE DRESSER
STEPIN FETCHIT

At the Hinner's Console—
RUSSELL
FIELDER
—presenting—
"EASTER SONG PARADE"
Featuring
LOUISE BROBERG

EXTRA: "THE FUNNY LITTLE BUNNIES"
ALL COLOR WALT DISNEY SILLY SYMPHONY HIT
PARAMOUNT SOUND NEWS   RICE SPORTLIGHT

MADISON

LOEW'S STATE
10TH CHAMPIONSHIP YEAR..
"Min and Bill" TOGETHER again!

STARTS FRIDAY

Marie (MIN)
DRESSLER
Wallace (BILL)
BEERY

AMERICA'S MOST LOVABLE SWEETHEARTS

"TUGBOAT ANNIE"

NRA MEMB. 2 U.S. WE DO OUR PART

with
MAUREEN O'SULLIVAN
ROBERT YOUNG

From the famous SATURDAY EVE POST STORY by Norman Reilly Raine

LOEW'S NOW!

"TOPAZE" RECEIVED 4 STARS IN THE LIBERTY MAGAZINE!

JOHN BARRYMORE

in

"TOPAZE"
He's a thief!

Adapted by Benn W. Levy from the stage triumph by Marcel Pagnol

with
MYRNA LOY

JOHN BARRYMORE IN THE ROLE HE CHOSE ABOVE ALL OTHERS ---

AN R.K.O. RADIO PICTURE

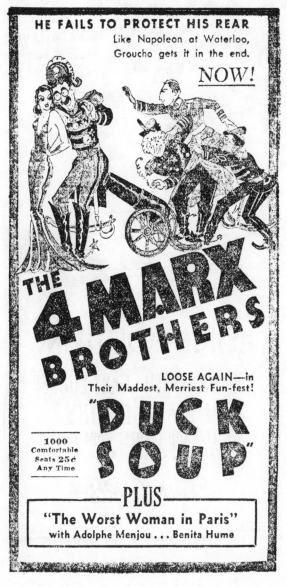

HE FAILS TO PROTECT HIS REAR
Like Napoleon at Waterloo, Groucho gets it in the end.

NOW!

THE 4 MARX BROTHERS

LOOSE AGAIN—in Their Maddest, Merriest Fun-fest!

1000 Comfortable Seats 25¢ Any Time

"DUCK SOUP"

PLUS

"The Worst Woman in Paris"
with Adolphe Menjou ... Benita Hume

WILLIAM BERKE presents
HARRY CAREY
in
"The LAST OF THE CLINTONS"

"Guilty As Hell" Today!
WITH
EDMUND LOWE
VICTOR McLAGLEN
RICHARD ARLEN
ADRIENNE AMES · RALPH INCE
PUBLIX APOLLO

PARAMOUNT
STARTS TODAY
Doors Open 11 A. M.
She Needed Two Men
1,000 SEATS 25¢ Anytime!
To fill her life . . . so the three of them kicked convention out of the window!

IT'S DARING But Hilariously Funny as Well!

Noel Coward's
"DESIGN FOR LIVING"
with
FREDRIC MARCH ★ GARY COOPER
MIRIAM HOPKINS
EDWARD EVERETT HORTON
A Paramount Picture
an
Ernst Lubitsch
PRODUCTION

AVON
TOMORROW!
Starts Tomorrow

Deliciously Naughty Romance!
When a siren and a he-man meet!
HONOR OF THE FAMILY
with BEBE DANIELS
More Beautiful Than Ever!
WARREN WILLIAM
He's Every Girl's Midsummer Night's Dream.

1st National & Vitaphone Hit! Splendid Extra Units
'Red' Grange in "The Galloping Ghost"
Booth Tarkington's "Snakes Alive"

STARTING TODAY!
- the two best-loved characters on the Screen!

Marie DRESSLER
Lionel BARRYMORE
Her SWEETHEART [CHRISTOPHER BEAN]

A Grand Picture! It will tug at your heartstrings . . . make you laugh till tears roll down your cheeks! You'll love it!

198

Edw. G. ROBINSON
Kay FRANCIS

TOMORROW
Lips of
Thunder
on Lips
of Fire!

Love Swept Them to the
Desperate Destiny of
Those Who Play Against
The Rules!

A Combination The Devil
Himself Couldn't Top! The
Irresistible Woman Meets
the Immovable Man!

IMAGINE ..

The Clash, the Drama,
the EXPLOSION when
she whispers at last that
she loves him . . . AND
MANY OTHER MEN!

"I LOVED A WOMAN"

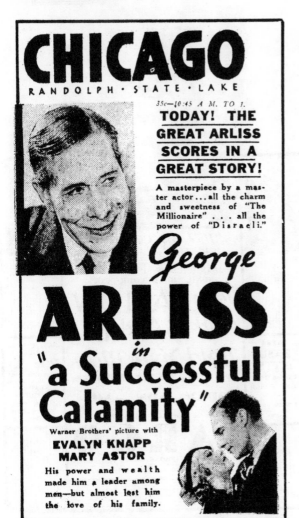

CHICAGO
RANDOLPH · STATE · LAKE

35c—10:45 A. M. TO 1.

TODAY! THE GREAT ARLISS SCORES IN A GREAT STORY!

A masterpiece by a mas-
ter actor...all the charm
and sweetness of "The
Millionaire" ... all the
power of "Disraeli."

George
ARLISS
in
"a Successful Calamity"

Warner Brothers' picture with
**EVALYN KNAPP
MARY ASTOR**

His power and wealth
made him a leader among
men—but almost lost him
the love of his family.

*Colman's most magnificent performance . . a dual
personality role that will live long in your heart!*

RONALD COLMAN
Elissa Landi IN

the MASQUERADER

SAMUEL GOLDWYN'S
swift-moving
romantic drama!

A UNITED ARTISTS
picture!

Extra!
SILLY SYMPHONY
"THREE LITTLE PIGS"

BALABAN & KATZ
UNITED ARTISTS
RANDOLPH AT DEARBORN

200

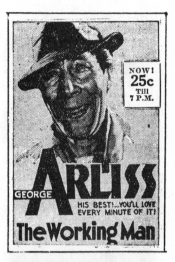

201

Made for LOVERS Young & Old

ONE HE LOVED...
ONE HE MARRIED!

He held his wife in his arms . . . and thought of the girl he might have had . . . Continually comparing the girl he did marry with the one he didn't!

"ONE SUNDAY AFTERNOON"

It'll take you back to your courtin' days . . . a tender, true romance with . . . . .

Gary **COOPER**

Fay Wray
Neil Hamilton
Frances Fuller
Roscoe Karns

Come With Someone You Love
STARTING TODAY

NRA MEMBER U.S. **WE DO OUR PART**

MISSOURI

ADDED ENJOYMENT
JACK HALEY
in an uproarous comedy
"Nothing but the Tooth"
Plus Walt Disney's cartoon successor to "Three Little Pigs"
"LULLABY LAND"
25c till 2 P. M.

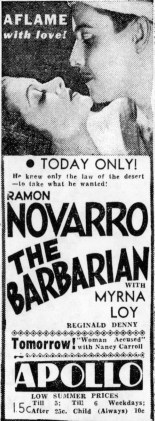

AFLAME with love!

● **TODAY ONLY!**
He knew only the law of the desert —to take what he wanted:
RAMON NOVARRO
THE BARBARIAN
WITH MYRNA LOY
REGINALD DENNY
Tomorrow! "Woman Accused" with Nancy Carroll

APOLLO

LOW SUMMER PRICES
Till 5; Till 6 Weekdays;
1.5c After 25c. Child (Always) 10c

TOMORROW

A Great Star
with a
A Great Cast
in a
A Great Story!
LIONEL BARRYMORE
in
"ONE MAN'S JOURNEY"
with
MAY ROBSON
DOROTHY JORDAN
JOEL McCREA
FRANCES DEE
—Extra—
"Hot Money"
Actual Trial of
URSCHEL KIDNAPPERS
First Time Shown!
—Also—
"Strange As It Seems" Novelty   News

MADISON

30c Till 6 P. M. After 40c
Child 10c. Dial 4-4901

202

● TODAY!
FOR 3 BIG DAYS!
Run for Your Wives . . .
Hold Your Sweethearts
Here's The Goofiest
Gob On The Seas
JOE E.
BROWN
in
SON OF A SAILOR
JEAN MUIR

THE DARING
THUNDERING
EPIC of AMERICA!
Timely! Sensational! Smashing!

WASHINGTON
MERRY-GO-ROUND

LEE
TRACY
CONSTANCE CUMMINGS
Alan Dinehart   Walter Connolly
Directed by James Cruze

A
COLUMBIA
PICTURE

TODAY! FOR THREE DAYS
DIAL 4-4901
MADISON
. . . One night of
heaven in her
arms! Snatched
from the Hell of
War!
COMRADES in the clouds!
ENEMIES on the ground!
Facing danger together—
for a lovely woman's smile!
A man's picture, that
women will love!

"THE EAGLE
and
THE HAWK"
with
FREDRIC MARCH
CAROLE LOMBARD
Jack Oakie   -   Cary Grant
● ALSO ●
"Mush and Milk"—Comedy.
"Workers of the World"—Novelty
Paramount News   Cartoon

25c
to 2 P. M.
35c
to 6. P. M.
Daily

She Promised to
Wait Two Years
—But That's a
Long Time!
RICHARD
DIX
in
"DAY of RECKONING"
CONWAY TEARLE
MADGE EVANS
UNA MERKEL
STUART ERWIN

METRO-
GOLDWYN-
MAYER
PICTURE

1934

It Happened One Night won the Academy Award as best picture of the year, with awards for Clark Gable and Claudette Colbert for their performances. Fred Astaire and Ginger Rogers danced their way through the best musical picture of the year, *The Gay Divorcee.* A young newcomer, Robert Taylor was playing the juvenile lead in the Will Rogers picture *Handy Andy.* Cecil B. DeMille's production for the year was the elaborate costume spectacle *Cleopatra,* with Claudette Colbert and Henry Wilcoxon. Marie Dressler died on July 28 and Douglas Fairbanks appeared in his last picture *The Private Life of Don Juan.*

CECIL B. DeMILLE'S "FOUR FRIGHTENED PEOPLE"
with
CLAUDETTE COLBERT
HERBERT MARSHALL
MARY BOLAND
WILLIAM GARGAN
A Paramount Picture

SUNDAY AND MONDAY

IT'S A FIELD'S DAY OF FUN!

W.C. FIELDS in "You're Telling Me"

with
LARRY 'Buster' CRABBE
JOAN MARSH
ADRIENNE AMES

a Paramount Picture

Improve your game and disposition at the same time by watching W. C. FIELDS play the 19th hole.

See Them Dance the
CARIOCA

The dance sensation of the hour! The musical hit of the minute! . . . See it! . . . Hear it! . . . Hum it!

FLYING DOWN TO RIO

RKO-Radio's smash hit with

DOLORES DEL RIO

Gene Raymond   Ginger Rogers
Fred Astaire   Raul Roulien
AND THOSE
200 BEAUTIFUL GIRLS
TANTALIZING TUNES BY
VINCENT YOUMANS

THE DANCE-MAD MUSICAL
The King and Queen of "Carioca" . . .
rhythmic stars of "Flying Down to Ri
bring you the most sumptuous rom
hit of all the seasons! . . . . The stage
triumph that ran for 248 glittering nights on Broadway and
thrilled London for six months! . . No
ten times more gorgeous on the scre
FRED ASTAIR
and
GINGER ROGE
in
"THE GA
with
ALICE BRADY
EDWARD EVERETT HOR
And Half the Beauties of Holl

UMPH OF TWO CONTINENTS!
See them do
"THE CONTINENTAL"
("You kiss while you're dancing!") . . . the tantalizing new dance sensation that races on flying feet down a rainbow of rhythm!
DIVORCEE"
Already the whole U.S.A. is whistling these new enchanting tunes:
"Don't Let It Bother You" and "Let's Knock K-neez", by Mack Gordon and Harry Revel.
"Looking for a Needle in a Haystack" and "The Continental", by Con Conrad and Herb Magidson.
Cole Porter's unforgettable "Night and Day", the stage show's glorious big song hit!
Directed by Mark Sandrich
Dances directed by Dave Gould
RKO RADIO PICTURE
Pandro S. Berman Production

Armed with a Doctor's Kit—
He Fought a Thousand Killers!
TOMORROW!
PAUL
MUNI
Dr. SOCRATES
WITH ANN DVORAK
EXTRA—
'MANUAL HIGH REVUE'
On Stage Mon. and Tues. Nights
ALSO
Short Features
PALACE
20c Till 6; After, 30c; Child 10c

WILL ROGERS
IRVIN S. COBB'S
"JUDGE PRIEST"
with TOM
BROWN · LOUISE
ANITA
ROCHELLE HENRY B.
HUDSON · WALTHALL
DAVID and STEPIN
LANDAU · FETCHIT
Produced by
SOL M. WURTZEL
Directed by
JOHN FORD
FOX

GLAMOROUS...
FASCINATING...
Anna Sten
in
"NANA"
As the Parisian daughter of
voluptuousness from Zola's
magic pages, she has a role
magnificently matching her
superb artistry. America
awaits, with expectant thrill,
this, her first American picture.

Tomorrow 9 a.m.

THE FLEET'S IN—THE FUN'S ON!

Here they come! Guns barking .. fists flying .. hearts pounding as 10,000 gobs come ashore to laugh, live, and love .. as only young sailors can!

"HERE COMES THE NAVY"

Two heart breakin', chin bustin' Irishmen nearly sinking a battleship and crashing a dirigible in their private war for a gal.

Warner's Thrilling spectacle
JAMES CAGNEY
PAT O'BRIEN

FRANK McHUGH • **GLORIA STUART**
And a Mighty Armada of The World's Greatest Fighting-Men

SEE . . . . the daring DIRIGIBLE RESCUE !

BALABAN & KATZ
ROOSEVELT
STATE NEAR WASHINGTON

THE GREATEST SHOW VALUE IN TOWN!

TODAY!
From the Famous 'Liberty' Magazine Serial by
ERLE STANLEY GARDNER

"THE CASE OF THE
HOWLING DOG
WARREN WILLIAM
MARY ASTOR

TODAY! FOR TWO ROMANTIC DAYS

...Of Course He's Naughty!
But that's the way you love him best!
Maurice flirting, fooling, singing, in gay Paree!

Maurice
CHEVALIER
IN
"THE WAY TO LOVE"
with ANN DVORAK
EDWARD EVERETT HORTON
—ALSO—
ANDY CLYDE in "Frozen Assets"
"WHAT PRICE SEED?"—NOVELTY
NEWS EVENTS

NRA
PALACE
NRA

20c Till 2 P. M. Sunday; Till 6 P. M. Weekdays; After, 30c.
Children 10c.   Dial 4-5901

UNITED ARTISTS
DEARBORN AT RANDOLPH

Open 8:45 a.m. Price change 1 and 6 p.m.
Blossoming in the Blush of a First Innocent Kiss . . .

Anna STEN
Fredric MARCH

in the Samuel Goldwyn Presentation of
"WE LIVE AGAIN"
EXTRA!
LAUREL and HARDY

210

ALL THE SPEED
...FIRE...COLOR
OF DOUG'S BEST!

Duels or dames...a
fight or a frolic...that's
Doug in this rollicking
tale cut from the glorious
pattern of "Zorro"...
"Don Q"..."Robin Hood"!
Welcome back, Doug!

HY
RUBIN

LONDON FILMS PRESENT

Douglas
FAIRBANKS
in ALEXANDER KORDA'S production of
The Private Life of
DON JUAN
with
Merle Oberon · Benita Hume · Binnie Barnes
and the Beautiful Ladies of "Henry VIII"
Released thru UNITED ARTISTS

212

W.C. **FIELDS** *in* **It's A Gift**

with **BABY LE ROY**

Without question the funniest picture in years . . . You'll laugh until you cry . . .

Starts Wednesday!
FORCED BY HER HUSBAND TO LOVE ANOTHER MAN —

—to exchange her kisses for naval secrets!

"**THUNDER IN THE EAST**"

with

MERLE OBERON

(Star of "Folies Bergere" and "Scarlet Pimpernel")
CHARLES BOYER
JOHN LODER
And a Cast of Many 1000's
United Artists Picture

25 TILL 2PM

TODAY! FOR FOUR DAYS

Gable As A Dashing Rogue Who Could "Dish It Out" And Could "Take It", Too!

One offered gaiety and excitement, the other, position and wealth.

Clark **GABLE**
William **POWELL**
Myrna **LOY**

Produced by
DAVID O. SELZNICK

Directed by
W. S. VAN DYKE

MANHATTAN MELODRAMA

Sensational Metro's Drama

• ALSO •
'OUR GANG'
in "FOR PETE'S SAKE"
PARAMOUNT SOUND NEWS

AT THE HINNERS CONSOLE
RUSSELL FIELDER
Presenting — THREE BRA-SHEAR SISTERS in "When My Dreams Come True"

PUBLIX GREAT MADISON STATES THEATRE

THE MOST FASCINATING LOVER EVER KNOWN!

Fredric March

Women succumb to his lure! . . . Men tremble before him!
—*in*—

"**DEATH TAKES A HOLIDAY**"

with
Evelyn Venable

WHAT DID THIS → *Woman Doctor*
LEARN ABOUT MEN?

"I'VE LISTENED TO A THOUSAND SECRETS THAT SHOULD MAKE ME HATE THE SIGHT OF MEN!"

SHE SAW WHAT LOVE COULD DO TO A WOMAN...BUT DECIDED IT WAS WORTH IT!

WHY DIDN'T THIS WO-MAN PHYSICIAN TAKE THE SAME ADVICE SHE GAVE TO OTHER GIRLS? See why she told her lover to marry another woman! See why she went to Paris...when she didn't have to! See how she paid for the sin she taught other women to laugh at!
DON'T MISS this great love drama of a woman who knows men for what they really are...

"MARY STEVENS M.D."

A woman's picture all men will understand...with

KAY FRANCIS

LYLE TALBOT ✦ GLENDA FARRELL
THELMA TODD ✦ UNA O'CONNOR

He a fugitive from the law... she fugitive from love. He crashed into her heart! And then they both discovered there was no escape... from conscience!

ROBERT MONTGOMERY
Fugitive LOVERS

with
MADGE EVANS
Ted Healy, Nat Pendleton

TODAY!
FOR 3 DAYS

20c Till 2 P. M. (Sun.). Till 6:00 week days; after, 30c. Child 10c. Dial 4-5901. Cont. 1 till close.

—ALSO—
Short Subjects

PALACE

TOGETHER AGAIN!..
for the first time since "Back Street"

IRENE DUNNE
JOHN BOLES
in
Edith Wharton's world-loved story of a rebel heart.

"The AGE OF INNOCENCE"

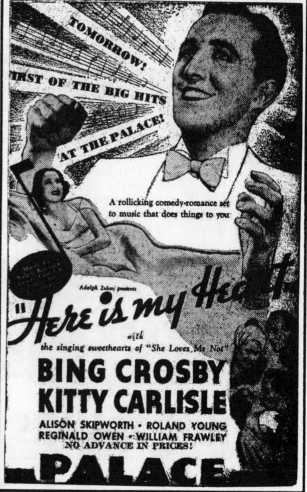

OUTLAWED BY MEN ... SOUGHT BY WOMEN!
What a liar! What a lover! What a rogue!

20th Century's boisterous drama!

Barg. Mat.
10:15 to 3

One hand at
every man's
throat .. the
other around
every woman's
waist!

Fredric   Constance
MARCH • BENNETT
"The AFFAIRS
OF CELLINI"
FRANK MORGAN—FAY WRAY

EXTRA
LAUREL
& HARDY
'Going Bye Bye'
Comedy riot

UNITED ARTISTS   RANDOLPH AT DEARBORN

McVICKERS
MADISON NEAR STATE

Op. 8:45 Pr.Chg.1 & 6
Plundered riches!
Stolen romance!
WALLACE
BEERY
"Viva
VILLA"
MGM's smash with
FAY WRAY
STUART ERWIN
LEO CARRILLO
and mighty
cast of
10,000

Today
FOR THREE
HAPPY DAYS

DICK POWELL
AND GINGER
ROGERS SING
THEIR WAY
STRAIGHT TO
YOUR HEART!

"20
MILLION SWEETHEARTS"

with
DICK POWELL • GINGER
ROGERS • PAT O'BRIEN
FOUR MILLS BROTHERS
TED FIORITO & HIS BAND
THREE RADIO ROGUES
— ALSO —
"Those Wonderful Days"—Cartoon
"Good Shape"—Sport Hit   News

PUBLIX
GREAT MADISON

TODAY! FOR FOUR MORE DAYS -- THE BIG HIT!
"WE'RE NOT DRESSING"
with
"LOVE THY NEIGHBOR"
Bing Crosby
CAROLE LOMBARD
GEORGE   GRACIE
BURNS & ALLEN
ETHEL MERMAN
LEON ERROL

MADISON

30c Till 6 p.m.; 40c
after; Child 10c

PARAMOUNT

★★★★
4 STARS
in LIBERTY Magazine

Today

1500 SEATS
25¢

The
MOST GLORIOUS
MUSICAL ROMANCE
OF ALL TIME!

"An Evening for the Gods"
says Photoplay Magazine.

MARY PICKFORD says . . . "Delightful Entertainment!"

A FEAST OF
LOVE, LAUGHTER
and MUSIC

Grace Moore
in
ONE NIGHT
of LOVE
WITH
TULLIO CARMINATI
Mona Barrie ── Lyle Talbot
A Columbia Picture ──

DAMES

Warner Bros.
Smash With
RUBY KEELER
DICK POWELL
JOAN BLONDELL
GUY KIBBEE
ZASU PITTS
and Many
Beautiful Dames

She'll steal your heart away—like "Lady For A Day"

Carole
LOMBARD · May ROBSON
in
LADY BY CHOICE
with Roger Pryor   Walter Connolly

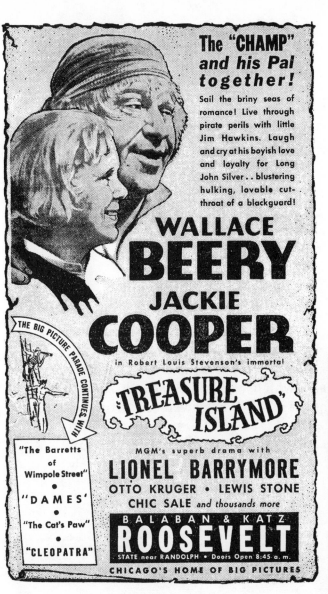

The "CHAMP" and his Pal together!

Sail the briny seas of romance! Live through pirate perils with little Jim Hawkins. Laugh and cry at his boyish love and loyalty for Long John Silver . . blustering hulking, lovable cutthroat of a blackguard!

WALLACE BEERY
JACKIE COOPER

in Robert Louis Stevenson's immortal

"TREASURE ISLAND"

MGM's superb drama with

LIONEL BARRYMORE
OTTO KRUGER • LEWIS STONE
CHIC SALE and thousands more

THE BIG PICTURE PARADE CONTINUES WITH

"The Barretts of Wimpole Street"
•
"DAMES"
•
"The Cat's Paw"
•
"CLEOPATRA"

BALABAN & KATZ
ROOSEVELT
STATE near RANDOLPH • Doors Open 8:45 a. m.
CHICAGO'S HOME OF BIG PICTURES

EDDIE'S BIGGEST AND BEST MUSICAL!

EDDIE CANTOR
IN
KID MILLIONS

WITH
ANN SOTHERN
ETHEL MERMAN
BLOCK and SULLY
and
GOLDWYN GIRLS

CANTOR GOES HIGH, WIDE AND GANDHI . . . as the fate of a nation hangs on a safety pin . . . stooge for a sheik one minute . . . indigestion for a camel the next . . . surprises upon surprise . . laughter in a swirl of desert beauty.

The future branded him a hero . . . . the past a criminal!
BUCK JONES in "THE MAN TRAILER"

Better than "BACK STREET"!
Colbert in Fannie Hurst's
IMITATION OF LIFE

STARTS TODAY
ANOTHER OF THE YEAR'S BIG SMASH HITS

WHEN SHE'S IN HIS ARMS
. . It's the grandest thrill the screen can give!

Clark GABLE • Joan CRAWFORD in CHAINED

1935

In 1935, one-time leading man William Boyd made his first appearance as Hopalong Cassidy. George Arliss continued his long list of biographical roles in *Cardinal Richelieu,* and Clark Gable starred in *Mutiny on the Bounty,* which won the Academy Award as best picture of the year. The Marx Brothers were cavorting in their best comedy, *A Night at the Opera.* On August 15, Will Rogers was killed in a plane crash in Alaska. Also in this year, Greta Garbo did a remake of her silent film *Love* under the new title *Anna Karenina.*

TODAY and TOMORROW!
MEET THE HAPPY FOUR!
..in a carnival of fun..with a laugh a second..and a second laugh after that!

CARNIVAL

with **LEE TRACY — SALLY EILERS**
JIMMY DURANTE
ALSO
HARRY LANGDON in
"HIS BRIDAL SWEET"
CARTOON — TOPICS

PALACE

20c TILL 6 P. M.; AFTER, 30c.
CHILD, 10c — DIAL 4-5901

SAMUEL GOLDWYN presents

BARBARY COAST

MIRIAM HOPKINS
EDW. G. ROBINSON
JOEL McCREA

TOMORROW!
LIONEL
Barrymore
in
THE RETURN of PETER GRIMM
With Helen MACK

David Belasco's Greatest Play!
A troublesome man but a lovable ghost he returned from the spirit world to feed the flames of a young romance!

PALACE

JACK HOLT
ROARING TIMBER

TODAY FOR 5 DAYS

IF YOU WERE A MILLIONAIRE

You Couldn't Possibly Find More Happiness Than You'll Get from This Greatest Laff-fest to Ever Shake Your Sides!

"THANKS A MILLION"

DARYL F. ZANUCK'S
20th Century Musical Romance

A MILLION DOLLARS' WORTH OF STARS
A TREASURE OF GOLDEN MELODY
A WEALTH OF ROMANCE
RICH IN LAUGHTER

DICK POWELL

FRED ALLEN - ANN DVORAK
PAUL WHITEMAN - RUBINOFF
and His Orchestra and His Violin
PATSY KELLY, YACHT CLUB BOYS
RAMONA - BENNY BAKER

ALSO
POPEYE CARTOON
TRAVEL SOUND NEWS

30c Till 2 (Sun.); 6 Weekdays; After 40c. Child 10c

MADISON

STARTS **TODAY!**

DEPT. OF JUSTICE   BUREAU OF INVESTIGATION
                         REPORT:

WOW! WHAT A SITUATION! Here I am posing
as this dame's husband and hopping all over
the country trying to catch the rest of this
gang of jewel thieves! I'm telling you, boss,
it's really embarrassing - what with hotel
clerks giving me the glassy eye and these city
cops trying to horn in. I offered her a bribe.
to come clean but she gives me the laugh --
she seems to enjoy my predicament! *Mac*

*Thus starts a
most amazing
and unusual ad-
venture . . . . .
packed with sur-
prises and com-
edy situations!*

●

**YOU'LL
CHEER THIS
SHOW—AND
SEE IT AGAIN
AND AGAIN!**

MYRNA LOY ★ SPENCER TRACY
Whipsaw

HARVEY STEPHENS   ●   **WILLIAM HARRIGAN**

ORIENTAL
RANDOLPH NEAR STATE

25¢
TILL 6:30

GEORGE RAFT
"THE TRUMPET BLOWS"
A Paramount Picture
ADOLPHE MENJOU
FRANCES DRAKE

CIRCLE
Tomorrow and Monday

Jimmy breaking hearts, chins and speed records as a rough tough truck driver who doesn't know what a stop signal means!

JAMES
CAGNEY
THE ST. LOUIS KID

GEORGE O'BRIEN
in
Harold Bell Wright's
WHEN A MAN'S A MAN
with
DOROTHY WILSON
PAUL KELLY

PARAMOUNT

2 features

25¢
till 1 p.m.

TOMORROW
More Romantic Than His Famous "In Old Arizona"

Warner
BAXTER
With
KETTI GALLIAN
"UNDER THE Pampas Moon"

SEE
The Pulse-Stirring
COBRA TANGO

plus

EXPOSED!
The Private Lives of a Whole Town

"Party Wire"
With
Jean Arthur
Victor Jory

Last Times Tonight
SHIRLEY **TEMPLE**
"OUR LITTLE GIRL"

GREATEST OF ALL AIR ROMANCES!

Hard-boiled, lovable Wallace Beery in his most heart-warming role! With a cast of thousands in a saga of our flying aces that will make your heart loop-the-loop with its thrills, its laughs, its romance!

WALLACE BEERY
in
WEST POINT of the AIR
with
Robert Young
Maureen O'Sullivan
Lewis Stone James Gleason

Features:
1:32 3:35
5:38 7:11
9:41

ALSO
THELMA TODD — PATSY KELLY
in
"THE TIN MAN"
MICKEY MOUSE
in "THE DOG NAPPER"
PARAMOUNT SOUND NEWS

TODAY! FOR 4 DAYS

Metro Goldwyn Mayer

MADISON

223

"CHARLIE CHAN'S SECRET"

WITH

Warner Oland

Greetings and Salutations!

It's a pleasure for the Old Maestro and all the lads to play for the fast dancing of that old coin-tosser, George Raft, in this novel melody melodrama!...Yowsah!

Tomorrow!
For 3 Days

ENDS TODAY! "The Bride of Frankenstein" with Karloff

Adolph Zukor presents

GEORGE RAFT
BEN BERNIE
(AND ALL HIS LADS)

in

"STOLEN HARMONY"

with
Grace Bradley · Iris Adrian
— EXTRA! —
LAUREL & HARDY   in "Fixers Uppers"
MICKEY MOUSE   in "Two Gun Mickey"

MADISON

30c Till 2 Holidays; Till 6 Week Days; After, 40c—Child, 10c

HE'S BREAKING THE HEARTS OF THOUSANDS

every time he wraps his tonsils around that soul-stirring love ballad, "She Was an Acrobat's Daughter"!

. . . And that's only one of the feats Joe performs in his big Show of Shows! He's a dancer, singer, acrobat, clown—and he's surrounded with the greatest array of stars and girls and gags anyone could ask in one great picture!

JOE E. BROWN
in
"BRIGHT LIGHTS"

A First National Picture with
ANN DVORAK · WILLIAM GARGAN
PATRICIA ELLIS · THE 5 MAXELLOS

GEORGE   Gracie
BURNS ★ ALLEN

in

"HERE COMES COOKIE"

with
GEORGE BARBIER
Betty Furness

A *Mighty Warship* AT THE MERCY of a *Murder Fiend*

NOW! UNTIL MONDAY NIGHT

Sensation-Packed!

Sinister spies . . . romance and thrills on the waves. You've never seen a mystery so different!

"MURDER in the FLEET"

with

ROBERT TAYLOR
JEAN PARKER

TED HEALY · UNA MERKEL
NAT PENDLETON
JEAN HERSHOLT
ARTHUR BYRON
FRANK SHIELDS

M-G-M PICTURE

15¢ TIL 1
25¢ TIL 5
35¢ EVES

PARAMOUNT

I CAN'T GIVE YOU ANYTHING BUT LOVE, BABY!

TOMORROW!

. . . AND WERE THEIR FACES RED . . . . .

When she said "No" to princes and dukes . . . and a career . . . to sit on a bench in the park with a bag of popcorn and a plain ordinary mug!

If You Liked "It Happened One Night," You'll Rave About . . .

CLAUDETTE COLBERT in "The Gilded Lily"

WITH FRED MacMURRAY (THE SCREEN'S NEWEST "FIND") AND A BIG CAST

ADDED SCREEN ATTRACTIONS
TERRYTOON "The First Snow"
JOHN MEDBURY Travelaugh "Among the Cocoons"
PARAMOUNT NEWS

225

GIRLS!—SEE WHAT IT TAKES TO MAKE A MIDSHIPMAN!

Here's your "pass" to Annapolis' jealously guarded halls and quarters! See how our sailor boys from every state live and laugh and love. Catch the soul-stirring spirit that makes them the fighting heroes of the Seven Seas! And let Ruby show you what it takes to land a certain romantic midshipman as her sweetheart. It's no cinch—particularly when it happens to be an ex-Broadway jazz maestro who's out to give the Navy the razz!

The historic "Ring Dance"—greatest of all Annapolis festivals—is only one of the picture's colorful events!

There's something about a sailor—that makes this the grandest romance in months!

Sensational new Warren Dubin songs! 'Don't Give Up the Ship'; 'I'd Love to Take Orders From You'—'I'd Rather Listen to Your Eyes'

DICK POWELL • RUBY KEELER

"SHIPMATES FOREVER"

The Navy's 'Flirtation Walk'—with

LEWIS STONE • ROSS ALEXANDER
EDDIE ACUFF • DICK FORAN • JOHN ARLEDGE
Filmed at Annapolis by 'Flirtation Walk's' director—FRANK BORZAGE
A Cosmopolitan Production • A First National Picture

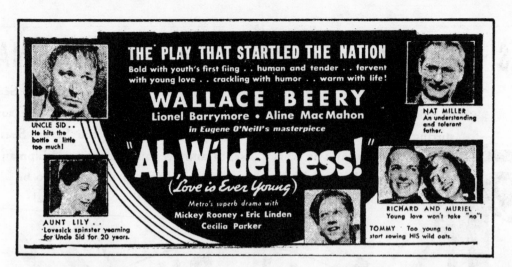

THE PLAY THAT STARTLED THE NATION

Bold with youth's first fling . . human and tender . . fervent
with young love . . crackling with humor . . warm with life!

WALLACE BEERY

Lionel Barrymore • Aline MacMahon

in Eugene O'Neill's masterpiece

"Ah, Wilderness!"
(Love is Ever Young)

Metro's superb drama with
Mickey Rooney • Eric Linden
Cecilia Parker

UNCLE SID ..
He hits the
bottle a little
too much!

NAT MILLER ..
An understanding
and tolerant
father.

AUNT LILY ..
Lovesick spinster yearning
for Uncle Sid for 20 years.

RICHARD AND MURIEL
Young love won't take "no"!

TOMMY Too young to
start sowing HIS wild oats.

PARAMOUNT

TOMORROW

THEY LIVE . . . . !

And you live with them . . . breath
for breath, thrill for thrill . . . because you are human . . . the story
is human—and humanity never
changes . . . in the air or on the
ground.

**MYRNA LOY
CARY GRANT**

in

"Wings in the Dark"

THE GIRL YOU LOVED IN "THE
THIN MAN," WITH MAE WEST'S
"BOY FRIEND" IN A CRAMMED-
WITH - ACTION ROMANCE OF THE
SKY DEVILS—

GALLANT HEROES

The Bengal Lancers,
handsome stalwarts,
often out-numbered,
never out-fought! The
thrill of a kiss, the joy
of combat...these, they
fight for...dangerously,
recklessly, madly!
Night finds them in the
warm arms of love...or
the cold clutch of death!

Adolph Zukor presents

"The Lives of a Bengal Lancer"

with

**GARY COOPER
FRANCHOT TONE
RICHARD CROMWELL
SIR GUY STANDING**

C. Aubrey Smith • Monte Blue
and Kathleen Burke

A Paramount Picture . . . Directed by Henry Hathaway

CHARLIE CHASE COMEDY
Ina Ray Hutton
"FEMININE RHYTHM"

★★★★
Four Stars from —
LIBERTY
MAGAZINE
"You may believe
anything the ads
say."

228

TO THWART A
KING'S PASSION
he gambled the fate of a nation

NOW!
Ends Sat.

Cardinal
RICHELIEU
starring
GEORGE ARLISS
with Maureen O'Sullivan

Tomorrow 8:45 a. m.
FIRST SHOWING!
EXCITING
in its swift action!
WHIMSICAL
in its chuckling humor!

It matches
thrill for
laugh . . .
romance for
escapade!

WILL ROGERS

All the genial character-
istics of Will Rogers in
this, his most enjoyable
role! Rich in wit . . in
laughs . . in
kindness!

Fox Film's
drama with
IRVIN S. COBB
ANNE SHIRLEY
EUGENE PALLETTE
STEPIN FETCHIT

STEAMBOAT ROUND THE BEND

ROOSEVELT
BALABAN & KATZ • STATE NEAR WASHINGTON

PRINCESS
Today! 5 DAYS
FIRST PEORIA
SHOWING!
DOORS OPEN 11:45 A. M.

Prices
Today:
20c Till 2
25c Till 5
30c After

Week Days
20c Till 6
25c After

HAPPINESS
AHEAD

DICK
POWELL
JOSEPHINE
HUTCHINSON
In Sensational 7-Star Cast

EXTRA!
Little Jack Little
In "At the Baby Parade"

A LITTLE GUY WITH A BIG HAT
TOMORROW! For 3 Days
Meet . . .
A cargo of human DYNAMITE
. . . a man who lived viciously
and . . . loved violently!

Ends
Today!
"School
for
Girls"
Sidney
Fox

4 HOURS TO KILL
with Richard
BARTHELMESS

EXTRA!
MICKEY
MOUSE
Cartoon in Color
"PLUTO'S
JUDGMENT DAY"

229

DEATH ON THE DIAMOND

Madge EVANS

Robert YOUNG

Nat Pendleton
Ted Healy

ON OUR SCREEN
Full length Feature
LAUREL
& HARDY *in*
"Bonnie Scotland"

A Romance as
Exotic . . . as Exciting
as a Cairo Night

"*The* LAST OUTPOST"

WITH
Cary Grant

Claude RAINS

Gertrude MICHAEL

Kathleen Burke

A Paramount Picture

25¢ TILL 1 PM

Last Times Tonight
Nino Martini 'Here's to Romance'
and "Wings Over Ethiopia"

STARTS TODAY!

Doors Open 10:45 A.M.

PRINCESS

Prices Today:
25c till 2 — 35c till 6
40c after 6
WEEK DAYS: 25c Till 6;
35c after 6. Children always 10c

Millions have seen it! Millions are seeing it! Millions more breathlessly await it—the picture that has made *Uncle Sam* the screen sensation of 1935——the sensational successor to "Here Comes the Navy"!

"DEVIL DOGS OF THE AIR"

JAMES CAGNEY
PAT O'BRIEN

MARGARET LINDSAY
FRANK McHUGH

A *Cosmopolitan* Production • A Warner Bros. Picture

THRILLS such as you've never known before as these flying leathernecks streak the flaming skies.

ROMANCE of the he-man, she-girl type that doesn't come in story-books —but is life itself.

LAUGHS—and you know the kind of laughs they are when Jimmy and Pat and Frank are handing them out.

—EXTRA ADDED ATTRACTIONS—
EL BRENDEL in "WHAT NO MEN"
Something Different in Comedy — Photographed in Color
—ALSO—
Freddie Rich and His Orchestra in 'Mirrors'

230

UNITED ARTISTS
RANDOLPH AT DEARBORN

You'll cherish this magnificent drama forever!

It's tender and stormy —triumphant and despairing!

FREDRIC
MARCH
CHARLES
LAUGHTON

Open 8:45; Pr. Chg. 1 and 6.
Features 9:05—11:15— 1:30—3:45—5:50— 8:05—10:20

In Victor Hugo's

Les Miserables

EXTRA!
MICKEY MOUSE
IN COLOR

20th Century's masterpiece
Rochelle Hudson, Frances Drake,
Cedric Hardwicke, John Beal

TODAY! ENDS SAT.

Sail Away on a Cruise of MERRIMENT and MELODY

"MISSISSIPPI"

with
BING CROSBY
W. C. FIELDS
JOAN BENNETT
QUEENIE SMITH

STARTING TODAY

"*Broadway Gondolier*"

Warner Bros.
Laugh Hit

DICK POWELL
JOAN BLONDELL
ADOLPHE MENJOU

STARTING
TODAY!

THE COMEDY STARS OF "DAMES"
IN A BIG HIT ALL THEIR OWN!

KANSAS CITY PRINCESS

JOAN BLONDELL • HUGH HERBERT
and GLENDA FARRELL

TODAY! FOR A WEEK

REGULAR PRICES — NO ADVANCE!

Dial 4-4901

MADISON

30c Till 2 (Sunday) Till 6 Weekdays;
After, 40c — Child, 10c All Times

TODAY: THEY'LL TAKE THIS TOWN BY STORM
...*fighting, laughing, loving
...breaking every law of the
seven seas bringing you the
screen's* MIGHTIEST THRILL!

CLARK GABLE has a new screen
sweetheart—lovely Tahitian Miamiti!

"MUTINY on the BOUNTY"

*The daring Bounty mutineers
who thrilled the world in the
SATURDAY EVENING POST STORIES!*

NOTE! First Performance
Starts at 12
(Noon) TODAY. Doors
Open 11:45. Features at 12,
2:28, 4:56, 7:24, 9:52.

ALSO
Betty Boop
In
"JUDGE FOR A DAY"

Paramount News

WITH
CLARK GABLE
CHARLES LAUGHTON
FRANCHOT TONE
Featuring A Cast of Thousands!
Metro-Goldwyn-Mayer's $2,000,000 Miracle Picture

3Uc Till 2 (Sun.)
Till 6 Weekdays;
AFTER 6, 40c;
Child Always 10c

MADISON

Today! For 4 Days!

CAGNEY LOVES!...CAGNEY HATES!
...CAGNEY TAKES!

He rules the seacoast of hell...the wildest,
lustiest mile on the face of the earth!

TODAY ONLY!
Doors Open 11:45.
Features at 12, 1:57,
3:54, 5:51, 7:48, 9:45.

JAMES CAGNEY

in the biggest of his 5 hits of 1935

"FRISCO KID"

A Warner Bros. Picture with

MARGARET LINDSAY
RICARDO CORTEZ
LILI DAMITA
1,000 MORE!

—ALSO—
March of Time
ALL NEW ISSUE
MICKEY MOUSE
in
"Mickey's Fire Brigade"

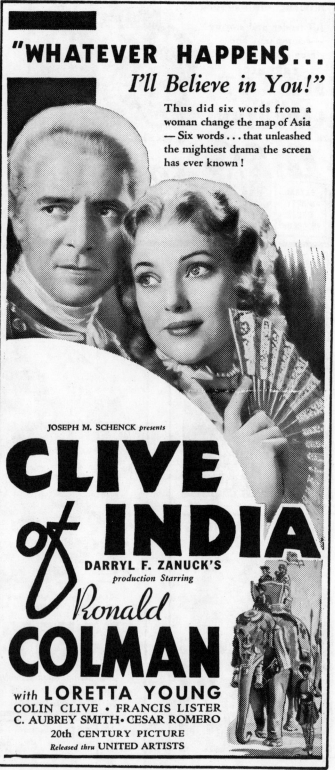

"WHATEVER HAPPENS...
I'll Believe in You!"

Thus did six words from a
woman change the map of Asia
— Six words...that unleashed
the mightiest drama the screen
has ever known!

JOSEPH M. SCHENCK presents

CLIVE of INDIA

DARRYL F. ZANUCK'S
production Starring

Ronald COLMAN

WITH LORETTA YOUNG
COLIN CLIVE · FRANCIS LISTER
C. AUBREY SMITH · CESAR ROMERO
20th CENTURY PICTURE
Released thru UNITED ARTISTS

The Sublime LOVE STORY!

Glorious Sweethearts together! Flooding your heart with the flaming ecstasy and bittersweet sadness of Tolstoy's impassioned romance! **TOMORROW!**

Last Times Today!
"THE GAY DECEPTION" with Francis Lederer, Frances Dee — Also "Dionne Quints."

MADISON

30c till 5 (Wed.); after, 40c; Child 10c

GARBO
Fredric **MARCH**
in TOLSTOY'S
"ANNA KARENINA"
with FREDDIE BARTHOLOMEW
M-G-M Cast

William **POWELL**
Ginger **ROGERS**
STAR OF MIDNIGHT

The "Thin Man" and the "Roberta" Darling Solve Amazing Crime!

What a cast for **LOVIN'.. FIGHTIN'.. ACTION!**

While typhoons rage . . . and blood-thirsty Malay pirates scuttle the ship . . . China Doll, silken siren of Shanghai, fights to hold her hard-boiled lover . . . lures the cold-hearted bandit chieftain with her warm caresses.

Metro's Thundering Melodrama

TOMORROW — 8:45 A. M.

**BALABAN & KATZ
UNITED ARTISTS**
RANDOLPH AT DEARBORN

CLARK **GABLE**
JEAN **HARLOW**
WALLACE **BEERY**
in
"china seas"

LEWIS STONE
ROSALIND RUSSEL
ROBERT BENCHLEY
EXTRA
MICKEY MOUSE
IN COLOR
"MICKEY'S GARDEN"

1936

In 1936, Tyrone Power had his first important role at Twentieth-Century-Fox in *Lloyds of London*. Joan Crawford, now one of Metro-Goldwyn-Mayer's biggest stars, appeared in *The Gorgeous Hussy* with James Stewart in one of his first screen roles. Universal released one of the big musical films of the year, *Show Boat* with Irene Dunne and Allan Jones. English child star Freddie Bartholomew co-starred in *Professional Soldier* with Victor Mc-Laglen. Ronald Colman played Sydney Carton in *A Tale of Two Cities* and Norma Shearer and Leslie Howard starred in *Romeo and Juliet*.

HELD OVER! for a few more days! **ENDS SUNDAY!**

LLOYDS OF LONDON

with 1937's New Star Discovery!

TYRONE POWER
MADELEINE CARROLL
FREDDIE BARTHOLOMEW
SIR GUY STANDING

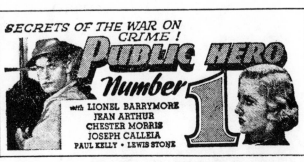

SECRETS OF THE WAR ON CRIME!

PUBLIC HERO Number 1

with **LIONEL BARRYMORE**
JEAN ARTHUR
CHESTER MORRIS
JOSEPH CALLEIA
PAUL KELLY • LEWIS STONE

STARTS TODAY

Gary **COOPER** *Mr. Deeds Goes to Town*

JEAN ARTHUR

HIS LOVE CHALLENGED THE FLAMES OF REVOLUTION...

The best loved picture of 1936 — made by the producers of "Mutiny on the Bounty" and "David Copperfield"!

"To the one I love—even though she loves another—I give all my love—and my life!"

RONALD COLMAN

A TALE of TWO CITIES

Metro's triumph from CHARLES DICKENS' novel

with **CAST OF 49,000**, including
ELIZABETH ALLAN • EDNA MAY OLIVER
REGINALD OWEN • BASIL RATHBONE
BLANCHE YURKA • HENRY B. WALTHALL

Tomorrow 8:45 a. m.

ROOSEVELT

BALABAN & KATZ   **STATE NEAR RANDOLPH**

235

THE MOTION PICTURE THAT IS
EAGERLY AWAITED THE WORLD OVER

Norma Shearer
Leslie Howard
in

Romeo *and* Juliet

with

JOHN BARRYMORE

EDNA MAY OLIVER · VIOLET KEMBLE-COOPER
BASIL RATHBONE · CONWAY TEARLE
REGINALD DENNY · RALPH FORBES
C. AUBREY SMITH · HENRY KOLKER · ANDY DEVINE

To the famed producer Irving Thalberg go the honors for bringing to the screen, with tenderness and reverence, William Shakespeare's imperishable love story. The director is George Cukor. A METRO-GOLDWYN-MAYER PICTURE.

You'll never laugh as long and as loud again as long as you live!

The laughs actually come so fast and so furious you wish it would end before you collapse!

You'll howl at Charlie's delirious antics as a factory hand!

You'll roar as you never have before when Charlie becomes the victim of the hilarious feeding contraption!

CHARLIE

Chaplin

in

MODERN TIMES

Written, Directed and Produced by CHARLES CHAPLIN • Released thru UNITED ARTISTS

Open 8:45 A.M. Price Change 1 & 6 P.M. Children Always 15c

UNITED ARTISTS
BALABAN & KATZ   RANDOLPH AT DEARBORN

You'll get the thrill of your life when CHARLIE SINGS!

237

"NO MAN WHO KISSES YOU ONCE WILL EVER BE CONTENT!"

AN UNBEATABLE CAST IN AN UNEQUALLED DRAMA!

What a "Gorgeous Hussy" is Peggy O'Neal .. five turbulent loves bring her ecstasy .. lead her recklessly into scandal .. her soft caresses threaten to topple a government!

JOAN AND BOB IN LOVE .. FOR THE FIRST TIME .. **WOW!**

Joan **CRAWFORD**
Robert **TAYLOR**
Lionel **BARRYMORE**
Franchot **TONE**
Melvyn **DOUGLAS**
James **STEWART**

in Metro's successor to "THE GREAT ZIEGFELD"

The "Gorgeous Hussy"

A CLARENCE **BROWN** PRODUCTION

A Metro-Goldwyn-Mayer PICTURE

ALMOST ALL HOLLYWOOD'S ROMANTIC STARS IN ONE PICTURE AND ... WHAT A PICTURE!

Not since "GRAND HOTEL" has there been a cast like this!

—EXTRA—
Cartoon In Color
Latest Pathe News

238

GARY COOPER · JEAN ARTHUR

Gary in the strongest role he's ever played, as Wild Bill Hickok, hardboiled hero of a thousand fights; Jean Arthur reaching new heights as Calamity Jane, hardboiled heroine of a thousand stories, living again, fighting again, loving again,.. amid the thundering terror of the last great Indian war.

Cecil B. DeMILLE'S "THE PLAINSMAN"

A Paramount Picture with JAMES ELLISON · CHARLES BICKFORD · HELEN BURGESS · PORTER HALL · Directed by Cecil B. DeMille

MEET THE WORLD'S GREATEST HIGH PRESSURE SALESMAN...
HE USES DYNAMITE

to break down his customers' sales resistance . . . . and make you collapse completely from laughter . . . . in a show that moved Film Daily to declare: *"again Joe E. Brown crashes through with a show that is a riot of fun. Loaded with gags, suspense, breath-taking hazardous situations!"*

JOE E. BROWN AS ALEXANDER BOTTS IN "EARTHWORM TRACTORS"

They're the stories that made millions roar in the Saturday Evening Post

A First National Picture with
JUNE TRAVIS
GUY KIBBEE
Dick Foran · Carol Hughes
Gene Lockhart · Joseph
Crehan · Olin Howland
Directed by Raymond Enright

RIVOLI

240

A SCREEN EVENT TO THRILL THE WORLD!!

GRETA **GARBO** *loves* ROBERT **TAYLOR**

in

Camille

Based on Authentic Facts by Famous Martin Mooney, the Reporter Who "Wouldn't Talk"! ★ The Most Important Crime Picture to Come to the Screen! Every Real Citizen Should See It!

EDWARD G. **ROBINSON**

in

BULLETS *or* **BALLOTS**

with

JOAN **BLONDELL** • FRANK **McHUGH**

BARTON MacLANE • HUMPHREY BOGART

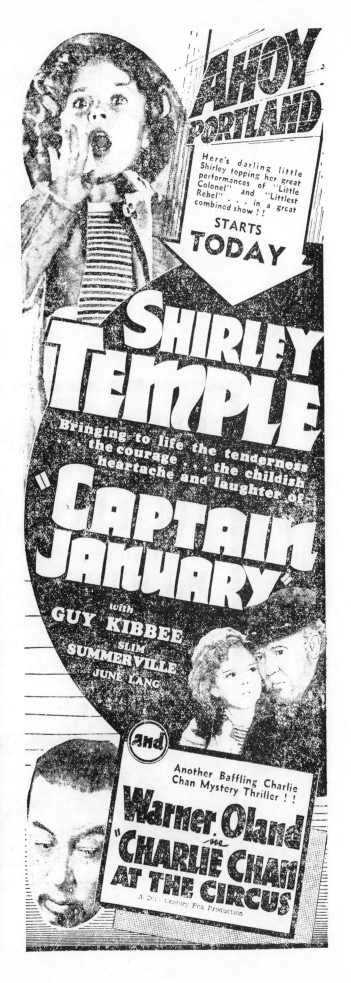

AHOY PORTLAND

Here's darling little Shirley topping her great performances of "Little Colonel" and "Littlest Rebel" . . . in a great combined show!!

STARTS TODAY

SHIRLEY TEMPLE

Bringing to life the tenderness the courage . . . the childish heartache and laughter of

"**CAPTAIN JANUARY**"

with

GUY KIBBEE

SLIM SUMMERVILLE

JUNE LANG

and

Another Baffling Charlie Chan Mystery Thriller!!

WARNER OLAND *in* "**CHARLIE CHAN AT THE CIRCUS**"

A 20th Century Fox Production

Love
as burning as Sahara's Sands

From Ouida's romantic novel of the French Foreign Legion, flashes this glorious spectacle-drama of men's heroism and women's devotion, enacted by one of the greatest casts the screen has ever seen.

UNDER TWO FLAGS
starring
Ronald
COLMAN
(Beau Geste)

featuring
Claudette
COLBERT
(It Happened One Night)

VICTOR
McLAGLEN
(The Informer)

ROSALIND
RUSSELL
(Rendezvous)

with GREGORY RATOFF • NIGEL BRUCE • C. HENRY GORDON • HERBERT MUNDIN

AND A CAST OF 10,000

a DARRYL F. ZANUCK 20th CENTURY PRODUCTION
(Les Miserables . . House of Rothschild)

Presented by Joseph M. Schenck
Directed by Frank Lloyd *(Cavalcade . . Mutiny on the Bounty)*
Associate Producer Raymond Griffith • Based on the novel by Ouida

Come Adventuring with

"CAPTAIN BLOOD"

The buccaneers are coming!...in Warner Bros.' vivid picturization of Rafael Sabatini's immortal story of the 17th century sea rovers.

After two years of preparation and, according to reliable Hollywood sources, the expenditure of a million dollars, "Captain Blood" is ready to furnish America with its big holiday screen thrill.

What with great ships, 250 feet in length, crashing in combat, with more than 1000 players in rip-roaring fight scenes—with an entire town destroyed by gunfire—this drama of unrepressed

THE PICTURE OF THE MONTH

hates and loves, the story of a man driven by treachery into becoming the scourge of the seas, is superb beyond any screen parallel.

And the cast is just as exciting as the production! First there's a brand-new star, handsome *Errol Flynn,* captured from the London stage for the title role; and lovely *Olivia de Havilland* who brilliantly repeats the success she scored in "A Midsummer Night's Dream". Others in a long list of famous names are Lionel Atwill, Basil Rathbone, Ross Alexander, Guy Kibbee, Henry Stephenson, Robert Barrat, and Hobart Cavanaugh, with Michael Curtiz directing for First National Pictures.

To do justice with words to the fascination of "Captain Blood" is impossible. See it! It's easily the month's grandest entertainment. And Warner Bros. deserve our thanks for so brilliantly bringing alive a great epoch and a great story!

Hollywood Does A Mirthful Martial Musical Up 'Brown'

JOE E. BROWN joins the army and 'slays' the world as the head man of a riotous regiment of singing

"SONS O' GUNS"

Including Joan BLONDELL

Beverly Roberts, Eric Blore, Winifred Shaw, Craig Reynolds, Joseph King, Robert Barrat

Those thousands of "Bright Lights" audiences who demanded another song-and-dance show for Joe have had their way! Warner Bros. went right out and bought that famous stage musical 'Sons O' Guns,' equipped it with an uproarious cast and all modern conveniences including new Warren and Dubin songs, and a passionate apache dance number by Joe that stops the show. The riotous results emerge as the month's top entertainment.

TAKE A BOW, LLOYD BACON, FOR YOUR DIRECTION

And the Same To You, Warren & Dubin, for These Great Songs

"A Buck And A Quarter A Day", "Put On A Uniform", "In The Arms Of An Army Man"

THE PICTURE OF THE MONTH

ROMANCE AND GAY ADVENTURE RIDE AGAIN IN M. G. M.'S MIGHTY SUCCESSOR TO "VIVA VILLA." You will thrill as Joaquin Murrieta, colorful bandit of old California . . . leaps to life from history's flaming pages!

Nights of Revelry and Romance . . . Days of High Adventure . . as Joaquin Murrieta with a woman at his side and a blazing six-shooter in his hand sweeps across the screen, the most colorful figure of California's daring days!

★

. . . His true life story now the screen's greatest entertainment. One year in production. Cast of thousands. Filmed on actual locations of Murrieta's exploits. Six towns rebuilt and populated.

Warner BAXTER in "ROBIN HOOD OF EL DORADO"

Ann Loring · MARGO · BRUCE CABOT

STARTS
Today

LESLIE
HOWARD
BETTE
DAVIS
The Unforgettable Lovers of
"Of Human Bondage" Reunited In
'PETRIFIED
FOREST'

Now Playing
Till Tuesday Night!

The picture
every woman
will want some
man to see !!!

Daringly
Intimate —
It's strictly adult
entertainment!

**Kay
FRANCIS**
George Brent
IN "
Give
ME
YOUR
HEART"

with
ROLAND YOUNG

And—
CHARLIE RUGGLES
MARY BOLAND IN
"WIVES NEVER
KNOW"

with
ADOLPHE
MENJOU

★ ═ TODAY! ═ ★

THE LIGHT BRIGADE CHARGES
ACROSS THE PARAMOUNT
SCREEN in the BIGGEST MOTION
PICTURE EVENT
of 1936!

☆

Love Gloriously . . . thrill unforget-
tably, as the reckless Lancers sweep
you on and on in this supreme adventure . . . so that a woman's heart
might not be broken . . . so that a
brave regiment's colors might remain
forever unsullied!

"No man is lost . . . while
some woman still loves him"

The **CHARGE** OF THE
LIGHT BRIGADE

with the Stars of "Captain Blood"
ERROL FLYNN
OLIVIA deHAVILLAND
PATRIC KNOWLES   NIGEL BRUCE
HENRY STEPHENSON
A Warner Bros. Achievement

And—
THEY'RE FUNNIER
THAN EVER!!
**LAUREL
& HARDY**
"Our Relations"

247

1937

Paul Muni, now one of the biggest names in pictures, starred in the Academy Award winner *The Life of Emile Zola* and *The Good Earth* with Luise Rainer. Mickey Rooney appeared in his first Andy Hardy picture. Most theaters were now showing double-feature programs. Child star Bobby Breen made a series of musical films at R.K.O., and *Stage Door* boasted a cast of Katherine Hepburn, Ginger Rogers, Eve Arden and Lucille Ball. In this year, Jean Harlow died at the age of 27 while making her last movie, *Saratoga,* with Clark Gable.

STARTS THURSDAY!

THE SMARTEST MUSICAL SHOW EVER FILMED! THE GRANDEST SONGS EVER WRITTEN!

Irving Berlin's "ON THE AVENUE"

with DICK POWELL

Madeline CARROLL — Alice Faye
THE RITZ BROS.

A NEW Screwball Triumph
The Love-Life of two Aero-Nuts—
TOLD IN A BURST OF HOWLS!

WHEELER & WOOLSEY IN "HIGH FLYERS"

with LUPE VELEZ

APPLETON

2 BIG FEATURES ★

Tonite: "Devil Is Driving" R. DIX and Jeanne Madden in "Talent Scout"

Starts FRIDAY

She'd say 'YES' — but she 'NO's' him too well

MARION DAVIES and ROBERT MONTGOMERY

And marriage proposals have been turned down for the same reason...

EVER SINCE EVE

All fun cast!

FRANK McHUGH
ALLEN JENKINS
PATSY KELLY
LOUISE FAZENDA

Plus:
Sally Eilers — Ricardo Cortez in "TALK OF THE DEVIL"
A baffling mystery!

Extra
PORKY'S BEDTIME STORY — Cartoon

PALACE Tomorrow!

The Big Fellow Is Out of ALCATRAZ! Ready to Show 'Em No Mercy!

"I'm going to pay them off .. going to make them sweat for every minute of the 10 years I spent on 'The Big Rock'!"

"Don't be afraid of him.. I love you.. and he can't do a thing to you!"

Edward G. ROBINSON in THE LAST GANGSTER

with
James STEWART • Rose STRADNER
Lionel STANDER • Douglas SCOTT
John CARRADINE • Sidney BLACKMER

ENDS TODAY!
"Wells Fargo"
Joel McCrea — Bob Burns — Frances Dee

—ALSO—
"SUNDAY NIGHT AT THE TROCADERO"
Comedy Howl
CARTOON   COMMUNITY SING

THEIR LOVE IS NEWS AGAIN!
...and you'd never forgive us if we didn't tell you—it's their perfect picture together!

Tyrone and Loretta...romancing in a new and more exciting way ...this time they really mean it with all their hearts!

TYRONE LORETTA
POWER · YOUNG

Second Honeymoon

Another hit from 20th Century-Fox
STUART ERWIN · CLAIRE TREVOR
MARJORIE WEAVER · LYLE TALBOT
J. EDWARD BROMBERG

Directed by Walter Lang · Screen Play by Kathryn Scola and
Darrell Ware · Based on the Red Book Magazine story by Philip Wylie
Associate Producer Raymond Griffith
Darryl F. Zanuck In Charge of Production

They parted in Reno....kissed impulsively under that Miami moon ...and the damage was done all over again!

20th
CENTURY
FOX

CIRCLE
TODAY and TOMORROW!
(One Main Feature Only)
A block that ends at the river's edge, where frustration lives, yet hope never dies! You may not like these people, nor pity them, but you'll never forget this picture!

Samuel Goldwyn
PRESENTS
DEAD END
starring
SYLVIA SIDNEY
JOEL McCREA
HUMPHREY BOGART
There's Never been a picture Hit Like This!

NOW PLAYING
"SURE, I LIKE A GOOD TIME!"

SAMUEL GOLDWYN presents
STELLA DALLAS

with
BARBARA STANWYCK
JOHN BOLES
ANNE SHIRLEY
Directed by KING VIDOR
RELEASED THRU UNITED ARTISTS

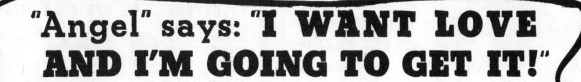

TOMORROW!
THE BOY STAR
OF THE YEAR...
IN THE
P I C T U R E
OF THE YEAR!

★

MICKEY
ROONEY
IN
"HOOSIER SCHOOLBOY"
with ANNE NAGEL · FRANCIS X. SHIELDS

ADVENTURE WITH "TRIGGER BILL!"

In a spectacular
romance of the wild,
golden West...with
the grand star of
"Viva Villa" bring-
ing pulse-pounding
thrills....heart-
warming laughs!

NOW!

THE
BAD MAN
OF BRIMSTONE
WALLACE BEERY
Virginia Bruce—Dennis O'Keefe—Lewis Stone

ALSO
OUR GANG
in
"FRAMING
YOUTH"
News   Sport

PALACE

Metro-Goldwyn-Mayer
presents a new and thrilling drama
by the authors of "San Francisco."
It is as exciting as the Sport of Kings
it dramatizes...and is the romance
of a daring gambler and a girl who
thought she wanted to ruin him.

CLARK
GABLE
J E A N
HARLOW
SARATOGA

with
LIONEL BARRYMORE
FRANK   WALTER   UNA
MORGAN · PIDGEON · MERKEL
Original Story and Screen Play by Anita Loos and Robert Hopkins
Directed by JACK CONWAY   Produced by BERNARD H. HYMAN
Associate Producer: John Emerson

A
Metro-
Goldwyn-
Mayer
PICTURE

ALSO
Color Rhapsody
INDIAN SERENADE
—
FITZPATRICK
Rocky Mountain
Grandeur
—
MOVIETONE NEWS

PALACE   NOW
PLAYING   30c to 2 Sun.: After, 40c; Child
10c to 5:30; After, 15c;
Weekdays, 30c to 6; After, 40c;
Child, 10c (All Day)

Out of the secret annals of the sea comes the strangest story ever told!

THE great Liverpool to Boston packet, burned to the waterline, plunges to her death in the grim waters of the mid-Atlantic. 25 men and women, after long, grueling days battling roaring seas in a life-boat return to tell their deathless story, a story so strange it has no counterpart in the turbulent history of the sea, a story which brings about the most sensational trial in maritime history, a story which inspires the grandest sea drama of them all, Paramount's thrilling action-romance, "Souls at Sea."

This is the greatest action picture of the greatest action director of them all . . . Henry Hathaway, who gave you "The Lives of a Bengal Lancer" and "The Trail of the Lonesome Pine."

GARY COOPER · GEORGE RAFT

"SOULS at SEA"

FRANCES DEE · Henry Wilcoxon · Harry Carey

DIRECTED BY HENRY "Bengal Lancers" HATHAWAY · A PARAMOUNT PICTURE

PARACHUTE KILLER PERILING PLANES!

You'll freeze in your seats when this crazed demon runs amuck 10,000 feet above the earth!

REPORTED MISSING!

with

WILLIAM GARGAN · JEAN ROGERS

A $1,000 BILL MADE A CHAMP OUT OF A CHUMP!

From the biggest boob in town, he became the most popular . . . and all because he still believed in Santa Claus!

EDWARD L. ALPERSON presents

STUART Erwin in "SMALL TOWN BOY"

AN ALL-AMERICAN LAUGH SPECIAL!

WARNER BROTHERS Proudly Presents—

Mr. PAUL MUNI

in one of the truly great pictures of all time ! ! !

The Life of Emile 'Zola'

with a cast of thousands . . . including

Gale Sondergaard
Joseph Schildkraut
Erin O'Brien-Moore
Donald Crisp

★ *LIBERTY Says*—
★★★★ 4 Stars—"It is genius colliding with life."

★ *TIME Says*—". . . It is one of the best shows."

★ *NEW YORK MIRROR Says*—"One of those extraordinary pictures which no one should miss."

The "must see" picture of the season is here! RKO-Radio's smashing screen sensation . . . from Edna Ferber and George S. Kaufman's laughter and heart throb stage success!

STAGE DOOR

Starring

KATHARINE **HEPBURN** ★★ GINGER **ROGERS**

ADOLPHE **MENJOU** with **GAIL PATRICK** . . .

CONSTANCE COLLIER · ANDREA LEEDS
SAMUEL S. HINDS · LUCILLE BALL . . .

Directed by GREGORY La CAVA · Produced by PANDRO S. BERMAN
Screen play by Morrie Ryskind and Anthony Veiller

The deep-down drama of those amazing girls who gamble everything for a thousand-to-one chance at footlight fame on Broadway. Their dreams, their hopes, their tragedies . . . told in a constant flow of flashing wit that breaks down all resistance. DON'T MISS IT!

STARTS TOMORROW!
The blazing drama of a beauty who climbed from the slums on a ladder of deceit and shame!

Joan CRAWFORD in THE BRIDE WORE RED with FRANCHOT TONE ROBERT YOUNG
A Metro-Goldwyn Mayer Picture

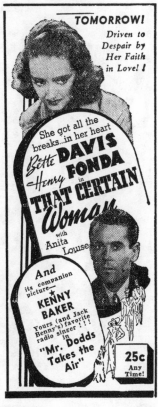

TOMORROW! Driven to Despair by Her Faith in Love!

She got all the breaks . . . in her heart
Bette DAVIS Henry FONDA in THAT CERTAIN Woman with Anita Louise

And its companion picture KENNY BAKER
Yours (and Jack Benny's) favorite radio singer !!! in "Mr. Dodds Takes the Air"

25c Any Time!

259

Stan LAUREL · Oliver HARDY

HAL ROACH STUDIOS Present

WAY OUT WEST

Also: "SWING FEVER"
Cartoon—Travelogue

Cool. Air-Conditioned

Liberty

STARTS TODAY!!

The "ONE in a MILLION" HONEY TOGETHER WITH THE SCREEN'S NUMBER ONE ROMANTIC STAR!!

The Magnificent Musical Romance You've Been Waiting for!!

Fidler Gives it 4 bells!

Filmed on Majestic Mt. Rainier

SONJA HENIE
TYRONE POWER
in *Thin Ice*

with
ARTHUR TREACHER
RAYMOND WALBURN
JOAN DAVIS

A Twentieth Century Fox Production

SUNDAY!

RIDING TO THE SCREEN ON A WAVE OF NEW LAUGHS!

3 MEN ON A HORSE

Warner Bros.' filming of the stage sensation, with

FRANK McHUGH
JOAN BLONDELL

GUY KIBBEE · CAROL HUGHES · ALLEN JENKINS
Sam Levene · Teddy Hart · A First Nat'l Picture
A MERVYN LeROY PRODUCTION

PRINCESS

DOORS OPEN 11:45 A. M.

• • TODAY FOR 4 DAYS • •

Old King Joe Crowns His Howling Career in This Story of a Palace Rave-olution!

A princess in danger and Joe in love! Swords clash! Women scream! Horses die laughing!

DAVID L. LOEW PRESENTS JOE E. BROWN

FIT FOR A KING

With
HELEN MACK
PAUL KELLY

An Edward Sedgwick Production.

Distributed by RKO-Radio Pictures.

260

AS PEARL BUCK WROTE--SO IT COMES TO YOU!

TERRIFICALLY ALIVE!!

The Two Years and the Fortune Spent, in Production Have created THE RANKING FILM ACHIEVEMENT!

An M-G-M Triumph!

See Every Character Every Scene as in the Book!

Forbidden Romance!
•
The Great Storm
•
O-Lan Before the Firing Squad

The Locust Plague!
•
Looting the Rich!

Affairs of Second Wife
•
Tryst With Sing-Song Girl!

"THE GOOD EARTH"

Comes to thrilling life, starring

PAUL **MUNI**
LUISE **RAINER**

with
WALTER CONNOLLY
TILLY LOSCH

★

ALL SEATS RESERVED
Shows Twice Daily!

Matinees 2:15
55c and 85c
Box Seats $1.10

Evenings 8:30
55c-85c-$1.10
Box Seats $1.65

400 GOOD RESERVED SEATS FOR ALL PERFORMANCES **55¢**

★

MAYFAIR

The GOOD EARTH
PEARL BUCK

STARTS FRIDAY!

SHE CLUNG TO HIM WITH FEVERISH DESPERATION
Hungry, for kisses that might end too soon . . . . Living, loving—as though any moment a vengeful world might tear him from her arms!!

WALTER WANGER'S THUNDERING DRAMA

Sylvia **SIDNEY**
Henry **FONDA**
IN
"YOU ONLY LIVE ONCE"

STARTS TODAY!!

☆

The academy award winner in the greatest two-fisted he-man role since his "What Price Glory?"

Victor **McLAGLEN**
IN
Sea Devils

WITH
PRESTON FOSTER
IDA LUPINO

AN R·K·O RADIO Production

261

1938

Color pictures were now appearing more often. Among the best of the year were *Tom Sawyer, The Adventures of Robin Hood* and *Kentucky*. Roy Rogers and Gene Autrey were the leading western stars in their pictures for Republic. Arthur Lake and Penny Singleton continued the popular *Blondie* series at Columbia Pictures. Harold Lloyd made one of his last films, *Professor Beware*. At this time, a family of four could have a night out at the movies and enjoy two features, a newsreel, cartoon, coming attractions, and perhaps the latest chapter of a serial, all for about $1.00.

JANET GAYNOR
Robt. Montgomery
FRANCHOT TONE

"THREE LOVES
HAS NANCY"

STARTS
Tomorrow!

MacDONALD • EDDY
GIRL of the
GOLDEN WEST

"SAN
QUENTIN'
with PAT
O'BRIEN
HUMPHREY
BOGART

Get set for red-blooded action
and amazing new thrills—the
screen now brings you sensational drama from behind the
walls of the world's most famous prison!

TO SET THE WHOLE
TOWN TALKING!!

One of the finest programs
the Paramount has ever presented. If you don't agree,
we'll gladly refund the price
of admission!
—The Management

AMERICA'S LITTLE
SWEETHEART MORE
ADORABLE THAN EVER!

Among all the
Shirley Temple
pictures this is
easily one of the
best for enter-
tainment!!

Shirley
TEMPLE
in
"LITTLE
Miss BROADWAY"

with
GEORGE MURPHY
Dancing Star of "Broadway Melody of 1938"
Edna Mae Oliver • Phyllis Brooks
Jane Darwell

HONOR and
TRADITION

Against
YOUTH
& LOVE!

A stirring
saga of the
old South!

KENTUCKY

with
LORETTA   RICHARD
YOUNG • GREENE

WALTER BRENNAN
Douglas Dumbrille

20th
CENTURY
FOX

in Technicolor

Also
Walt Disney's
DONALD
DUCK in
"Donald's
Better Self"

"Hang me? You can't hang a man till you've taken him!"

"The Redcoats! It's death if they find him!"

Heroic romance and adventure... as a valiant three defy a nation's vengeful might! The story the author of "Treasure Island" always considered his best... spectacularly told on the screen for the first time!

A 20th Century-Fox Picture. Pictorially enriched throughout with the glowing, new sepia-tone.

Robert Louis Stevenson's

Kidnapped

"Take me with you... no matter what comes!"

with a cast of 5000 featuring

WARNER BAXTER • FREDDIE BARTHOLOMEW

in his most dashing and colorful role!

in his first picture since "Captains Courageous!"

ARLEEN WHELAN

The year's emotional discovery in her star-role debut!

C. AUBREY SMITH • REGINALD OWEN

John Carradine • Nigel Bruce • Miles Mander
Ralph Forbes • H. B. Warner • E. E. Clive
Directed by Alfred Werker, Director of "The House of Rothschild"

★ **Paramount**

STARTS TODAY!!

IT'S FUN O'CLOCK MOUNTAIN TIME!
. . . and how the fun keeps mountin' up!
They LOOK Hillbilly . . . they TALK
Hillbilly . . . but don't let the whiskers
fool you . . . they're public maniacs Nos. 1,
2 and 3—in the consarndest mess of fun ever!

THE RITZ Brothers
IN
KENTUCKY Moonshine

with
TONY MARTIN
MARJORIE WEAVER
SLIM SUMMERVILLE

A 20th Century-Fox laff riot
produced by Darryl F. Zanuck

Clark **GABLE** · Myrna **LOY**
TOO HOT TO HANDLE

WALTER   WALTER   LEO
PIDGEON   CONNOLLY   CARRILLO

MADISON   A Love Story that
TOMORROW!   Packs Thrills!

Powerful, yet tender
drama! . . superb, vivid
performances merit
Academy Awards for
its great stars!

Robert **TAYLOR**
Margaret
SULLAVAN
Franchot   Robert
TONE · YOUNG
in
THREE COMRADES

with
Guy KIBBEE · Lionel ATWILL
Henry HULL · A FRANK BORZAGE
Production
Directed by FRANK BORZAGE
Produced by JOSEPH L. MANKIEWICZ

ENDS TODAY!
"MAYERLING"
with
Charles   Danielle
BOYER   DARRIEUX

W. C. FIELDS in "The BIG BROADCAST OF 1938"

with MARTHA RAYE DOROTHY LAMOUR

Plus so many stars and songs it takes a whole ocean to put on the extravaganza!

THE FINEST ARRAY OF ENTERTAINMENT EVER OFFERED!

through miles of raging ocean.. he defied man's law..A turbulent story of primitive passions by the authors of "Mutiny on the Bounty"

with
Dorothy LAMOUR · Jon HALL
Mary ASTOR · C. Aubrey SMITH
Thos. MITCHELL · Raymond MASSEY
Directed by JOHN FORD

THE HURRICANE

MADISON

THRILLING, BREATH-TAKING ACTION storms the screen! Tomorrow

CLARK GABLE

MYRNA LOY

SPENCER TRACY

Written by Peoria's Own Frank Wead

A VICTOR FLEMING PRODUCTION

THRILLS YOU'LL NEVER FORGET!

SEE...the Drake Bullet smash the coast-to-coast speed record.

SEE... the wings of a pursuit plane crumple at a speed of 8 miles per minute!

SEE...an Army bomber tested at a height of thirty thousand feet!

SEE...throttles opened wide in the National Air Races!

SEE...planes deliberately plunged to destruction!

TEST PILOT

with LIONEL BARRYMORE

ENDS TODAY! "IN OLD CHICAGO"
ALICE FAYE
Tyrone Power — Don Ameche

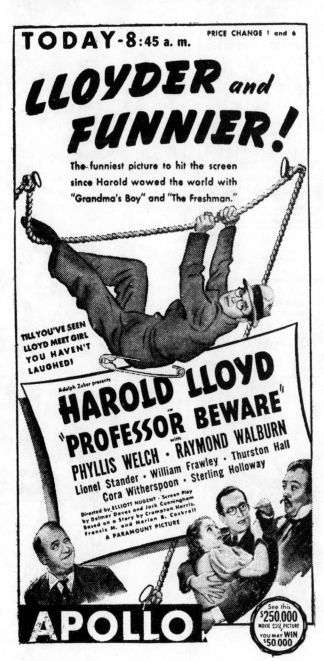

TODAY - 8:45 a. m.   PRICE CHANGE 1 and 6

LLOYDER and FUNNIER!

The funniest picture to hit the screen since Harold wowed the world with "Grandma's Boy" and "The Freshman."

TILL YOU'VE SEEN LLOYD MEET GIRL YOU HAVEN'T LAUGHED!

Adolph Zukor presents

HAROLD LLOYD "PROFESSOR BEWARE"

with
PHYLLIS WELCH · RAYMOND WALBURN
Lionel Stander · William Frawley · Thurston Hall
Cora Witherspoon · Sterling Holloway

Directed by ELLIOTT NUGENT · Screen Play by Delmer Daves and Jack Cunningham Based on a Story by Crompton Harris, Francis M. and Marion B. Cockrell
A PARAMOUNT PICTURE

APOLLO

See this $250,000 MOVIE QUIZ PICTURE YOU MAY WIN $50,000

NOW PLAYING
Jack Holt rises to new heights in this action hit!

JACK HOLT

THE STRANGE CASE OF Dr. Meade

AND SECOND FEATURE
Thrill-packed story of love and high adventure!

EDITH FELLOWS in **THE LITTLE ADVENTURESS**

LIBERTY
STARTS TOMORROW

BETTE DAVIS in **"Jezebel"**

with HENRY FONDA GEORGE BRENT

STARTS TOMORROW!
★

Three bright-eyed girls look for love ...and a man with a million dollars!

Thousands of girls (millions!) have had the same dream...but these three do something about it! Ah, romance... Oh, what fun!

Any girl can marry a poor man...but Loretta wants to learn how the other half loves!

Loretta **YOUNG** *Joel* **McCREA** in **THREE BLIND MICE**

with
DAVID NIVEN
STUART ERWIN
MARJORIE WEAVER
PAULINE MOORE
BINNIE BARNES
JANE DARWELL

Directed by William A. Seiter
Based on a play by Stephen Powys

When Pauline kisses, she keeps her eyes wide-open... at least she tries!

If Marjorie can't get a man *with* a million, she'll settle for a man *in* a million!

Sparkling, gay, romantic! Brilliantly produced by Darryl F. Zanuck and hit-making 20th Century-Fox!

THE PERFECT PICTURE STARTS

TODAY!

REGULAR CONTINU-
OUS PERFORMANCES
STARTING AT 11
A. M.

•

COME EARLY TO
AVOID THE CROWDS!

'We have been selected as one of
the First Few Cities in America
to show "Pygmalion". At the very
moment that New York and Los
Angeles preview audiences are
cheering Bernard Shaw's first au-
thorized photoplay — it comes to
this city while all America waits
to see it! It's the year's BIG entertainment event!

"I LOVE
IT TOO!"

**New York Critics Name
It Among the "Ten Best"**

'Pygmalion' magnificent!"
N.Y. Herald Tribune

"A grand show!"   *N.Y. Times*

"Drop everything and rush to see it!"
N.Y. World-Telegram

"Worth seeing twice!"   *N.Y. Post*

"Don't miss it!"   *Louella Parsons*

LESLIE

HOWARD

in

BERNARD SHAW'S

PYGMALION

with WENDY HILLER and
WILFRID LAWSON · MARIE LOHR · SCOTT SUNDERLAND
Screen Play and Dialogue by Bernard Shaw
Music by Arthur Honegger
Directed by Anthony Asquith and Leslie Howard
A Metro-Goldwyn-Mayer Picture · Produced by GABRIEL PASCAL

He picked up a girl from the
gutter—and changed her into a
glamorous society butterfly!...
See Wendy Hiller, new star discovery, in this amazing role!

LESLIE HOWARD
IN BERNARD SHAW'S
PYGMALION

Record crowds at New York's
Astor Theatre (now in its 3rd
month) and in Los Angeles
cheer this amazing hit!

269

Adolph Zukor presents

FRED MacMURRAY in

"COCOANUT GROVE"

HARRIET HILLIARD · RUFE DAVIS · THE YACHT CLUB BOYS
BEN BLUE · BILLY LEE · HARRY OWENS and His Royal Hawaiian Orch.

High Riding Romance!

AT THE RENDEZVOUS of the STARS!

PRICES
30c to 2; 40c
to 5:30; After
45c (plus tax) child
10c to 5:30; After, 15c

Hopalong Cassidy plunges into another adventure!

Adolph Zukor presents

CLARENCE E. MULFORD'S

"HEART of the WEST"

A Paramount Release with

WILLIAM BOYD
JIMMY ELLISON

George Hayes · Lynn Gabriel
Sidney Blackmer · Fred Kohler

His Love-Making was as Dangerous as His Sword-Play

Adolph Zukor presents

Ronald Colman

in FRANK LLOYD'S

"IF I WERE KING"

A Paramount Picture with

Frances Dee · Basil Rathbone

PALACE

THE LOVE AFFAIR THAT TOPS 'EM ALL!

Gary's

a romantic rover, who loves 'em and leaves 'em . . . till

Claudette

stops him cold . . . with her saucy, scandalizing technique!

30c to 2
(Sunday)
After 40c
Child 10c to
5:30; after
15c

Starting . . .

Today!

—ALSO—
"MEET THE MAESTROS"
—featuring—
Isham Jones   Phil Spitalny
Russ Morgan   Cab Calloway
        Clyde Lucas
NOVELTY   NEWS EVENTS

ADOLPH ZUKOR PRESENTS

CLAUDETTE COLBERT · GARY COOPER

"BLUEBEARD'S EIGHTH WIFE"

EDWARD EVERETT HORTON · DAVID NIVEN · ELIZABETH PATTERSON · HERMAN BING

Screen Play by Charles Brackett and Billy Wilder · Based on the Play by Alfred Savoir · English Play Adaptation by Charlton Andrews

PRODUCED AND DIRECTED BY ERNST LUBITSCH   A PARAMOUNT PICTURE

CASSIDY MEETS HIS MATCH!

Adolph Zukor presents

CLARENCE E. MULFORD'S "PARTNERS OF THE PLAINS"

featuring WILLIAM BOYD

Harvey Clark · Russell Hayden · Gwen Gaze
Hilda Plowright · John Warburton · Al Bridge

—plus—
"OUR GANG FOLLIES"
and
Other Units of SCREEN VAUDEVILLE

IT STARTS TODAY ON THE SCREEN It's a Riot!

Bella and Samuel Spewack's
BOY MEETS GIRL
(from the play produced by George Abbott)

JAMES   Together Again!   PAT
CAGNEY and O'BRIEN

CAPITOL
ALWAYS COOL
TODAY — 2 SCREEN HITS
Gene AUTRY
'ROOTIN' TOOTIN' RHYTHM'

DIRECTION OF JENSEN & VON HERBERG   FIRST AND PIKE MAIN 83¢
LIBERTY
HELD OVER!
• BETTER HURRY! •
POSITIVELY
LAST FEW DAYS!

FREDRIC
MARCH
VIRGINIA
BRUCE
in
THERE GOES
MY HEART

A MOVIE QUIZ
$250,000.00
CONTEST PICTURE

Plus 2nd FEATURE
JACK HOLT in
"Crime Takes A Holiday"

Starts TOMORROW!
It's All New!
It's All Different!

And
Meet fiction's modern
Robin Hood—brought to
thrilling life!!
Leslie Charteris'
"THE SAINT IN NEW YORK"
with LOUIS HAYWARD

"GOLD DIGGERS IN Paris"

with
RUDY VALLEE
ROSEMARY LANE
HUGH HERBERT • ALLEN JENKINS
THE SCHNICKELFRITZ BAND
Musical numbers created and
directed by Busby Berkeley

30¢ TILL 1
35¢ 1 TO 5
40¢ NIGHTS

Orpheum

Ends Tonight! "You and Me" Sylvia Sidney George Raft • And • "Change of Heart" Gloria Stuart Michael Whalen

PALACE

Tomorrow! Three's a Crowd! And What a Crowd!

ADOLPH ZUKOR PRESENTS

GLADYS SWARTHOUT
JOHN BOLES
JOHN BARRYMORE

in

"ROMANCE IN THE DARK"

A Paramount Picture with
CLAIRE DODD · FRITZ FELD · CURT BOIS

Hear
"Tonight We Love"
"Blue Dawn"
"Bewitched by the Night"

Ends Today Edw. G. Robinson
"Slight Case of Murder"

Kicking the pigskin for a skinful of laughs!

JOE. E BROWN

See this $250,000 DAYE ONE PICTURE
YOU MAY WIN $50,000

THE GLADIATOR

MAN MOUNTAIN DEAN
JUNE TRAVIS · DICKIE
MOORE · LUCIEN LITTLE-
FIELD · ROBERT KENT

STARTS TOMORROW!

★

For your convenience, note early time schedule!

"ALWAYS GOODBYE"
1:25, 4:05,
Evening
6:50, 9:35.

"PASSPORT HUSBAND"
11:55 A. M., 2:40,
5:25, 8:05, 10:50
P. M.

A WOMAN IN LOVE...

and her valiant struggle to win the happiness that is her woman's right...knowing she must choose forever between the man of her heart and the son she can never claim for her own! Drama fired with inspired performances...and the star of "Stella Dallas" at her greatest!

BARBARA STANWYCK
HERBERT MARSHALL

in

Always Goodbye

with

IAN HUNTER
CESAR ROMERO · LYNN BARI
BINNIE BARNES · JOHN RUSSELL

Directed by Sidney Lanfield
Associate Producer Raymond Griffith
Screen Play by Kathryn Scola and Edith Skouras
Darryl F. Zanuck In Charge of Production

A 20th Century-Fox Picture

HERE'S THE YANKEE CLIPPER HIMSELF!

A two-fisted terror from the States...
who landed in England with a chip
on his shoulder . . . but let a blue-
eyed beauty walk off with his heart!
BOB TAYLOR'S BIGGEST PICTURE HIT!

ROBERT TAYLOR
in
"A YANK at OXFORD"

MIDWEST PREMIERE!
8:45 a.m. Tomorrow

United Artists
BALABAN & KATZ • RANDOLPH AT DEARBORN *Hearing Aids*

LIONEL BARRYMORE
MAUREEN O'SULLIVAN • VIVIEN LEIGH
EDMUND GWENN • GRIFFITH JONES

His Greatest Picture

A4-
★ Western Thriller

"BAR 20 JUSTICE"

Another New
Hopalong Cassidy
Drama with
WILLIAM BOYD
Gwen Gaze and George Hayes

PALACE
TOMORROW!

Yelps in the Alps!

THEY'RE MOUSE-TRAP SALESMEN IN THE ALPS—and are the mice happy!

HAL ROACH *presents*
STAN LAUREL • OLIVER HARDY
in ## Swiss Miss
DELLA LIND • WALTER WOOLF KING
ERIC BLORE
Original Story by Jean Negulesco and Charles Rogers, Associate Producer
Directed by JOHN G. BLYSTONE
S. S. VAN KEUREN

ENDS TODAY!
"Crime School"
with HUMPHREY BOGART

Also: Eddie Grafton in 'Photo-grafters'

MADISON TOMORROW!

ENDS TODAY
"Three Comrades" Robt. Taylor Margaret Sullivan

The World's Most Beloved Rogues Live Forever on the Color Screen!

Most Thrilling Romantic Adventure of All Time!

The Adventures of
Robin Hood

ERROL FLYNN

OLIVIA DeHAVILLAND
BASIL RATHBONE
CLAUDE RAINS
PATRIC KNOWLES • EUGENE
PALLETTE • ALAN HALE
MELVILLE COOPER • IAN
HUNTER • UNA O'CONNOR

EXTRA!
HOME TOWN NEWS REEL
See Yourself and Your Friends on the Screen!

Direct From Its
Sensational Engagements
28 Weeks in New York
26 Weeks in Paris
20 Weeks in London
16 Weeks in Vienna
12 Weeks in Berlin
12 Weeks in Los Angeles.

Proudly we present the
international triumph—

Mayerling

with

BOYER
CHARLES

DANIELLE
D. ARRIEUX

The Hardy Family's newest!

LOVE FINDS
Andy **HARDY**

with

MICKEY ROONEY

Lewis Stone ★ Judy Garland
and a great M-G-M cast!

STARTS
WEDNESDAY!

SHIRLEY TEMPLE
in
**"REBECCA OF
SUNNYBROOK FARM"**

Roaring into each blood-red dawn
... fighting for women they had
never seen ... for love they might
never know!!

Errol **FLYNN**
as the Daring Leader of ...

**"THE DAWN
PATROL"**

with
BASIL RATHBONE
DAVID NIVEN

Extra
WALT
DISNEY'S
SILLY SYMPHONY
**"FERDINAND
THE
BULL"**

(In Technicolor)

Starts
Tomorrow!
★

**A TEAR...BEHIND
THE SMILE!!**

Out of the depths of a girl's heart
... and the vision of a boy's
dreams ... comes one of the
great romances of modern times
... so daring, so tender, so human,
so true ... that everyone in love
will want to see it!!

**CARY
GRANT
KATHARINE
HEPBURN**
in

"Holiday"
★

with
EDWARD EVERETT HORTON
LEW AYRES ★ DORIS NOLAN
A Columbia Production

And
Its Companion Picture—

RICHARD DIX
in
"BLIND ALIBI"

30¢ **35¢** **40¢**
TILL 1   1 TO 5   NIGHTS

You've Got A Date With Danger, A Rendzevous With Romance In The Glamerous, Mysterious Algiers..

MAKE A DATE NOW!

FRIDAY!

WALTER WANGER presents

Charles BOYER in ALGIERS

HEDY LAMARR
SIGRID GURIE

Released thru United Artists

LIBERTY

A MOVIE QUIZ $250,000.00 CONTEST PICTURE!

—Ends Tonight—
"Girl of the Golden West" and "Dangerous to Know"

STARTS WEDNESDAY!

A flaming romance in a city aflame . . . it's the spectacular picture of the year.

IN OLD CHICAGO

with

TYRONE POWER
ALICE FAYE

Don Ameche
Alice Brady

A 20th Century Fox Production

MADISON A NEW SEASON HIT!

THE BATTY BEEBES ARE ON THE LOOSE AGAIN!

YOU HAVEN'T REALLY LAUGHED

See this $250,000 MOVIE QUIZ PICTURE YOU MAY WIN $50,000

TILL YOU MEET THE BEEBES . . .

THE DARNDEST FAMILY IN THE U.S.A.!

When they're not singin' they're flingin' things at each other!

Adolph Zukor presents

BING CROSBY · Fred MacMURRAY

"SING YOU SINNERS"

ELLEN DREW · ELIZABETH PATTERSON · DONALD O'CONNOR

Original Story and Screen Play by Claude Binyon · A Paramount Picture

Produced and Directed by

WESLEY RUGGLES

30c to 2 (Sun. and Holidays); After, 40c; Child 10c to 5:30; After, 15c.

You'll love 'em when you hear 'em sing:

"Laugh and Call It Love"
"Pocketful of Dreams"
"Don't Let That Moon Get Away", "Small Fry"

MARCH of TIME ALSO All New Issue | DONALD DUCK in "The Fox Hunt"

ONE OF THE MOVIE QUIZ $250,000.00 CONTEST PICTURES

275

1939

After years of working in small-budget westerns, John Wayne hit the big time in John Ford's classic film *Stagecoach*. Al Jolson returned to the screen in *Rose of Washington Square,* while Warner Baxter was back in his famous Cisco Kid role. The Ritz Brothers made a wild musical comedy version of *The Three Musketeers*. Mickey Rooney was playing *Huckleberry Finn,* and once-famous star Richard Barthelmess was making a come back in a supporting role in *Only Angels Have Wings*. Charles Laughton starred in a remake of Lon Chaney's silent picture *The Hunchback of Notre Dame.*

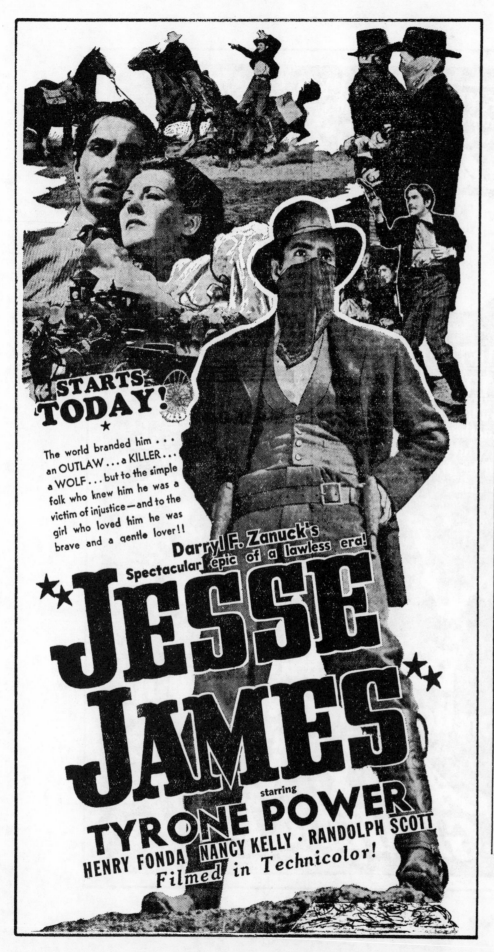

STARTS TODAY!
★

The world branded him . . .
an OUTLAW . . . a KILLER . . .
a WOLF . . . but to the simple
folk who knew him he was a
victim of injustice—and to the
girl who loved him he was
brave and a gentle lover!!

Darryl F. Zanuck's
Spectacular epic of a lawless era!

★★ JESSE
JAMES ★★

starring
TYRONE POWER
HENRY FONDA · NANCY KELLY · RANDOLPH SCOTT
Filmed in Technicolor!

Hedy Lamarr set the world
aflame with her beauty in
"Algiers"! Now you see her in
the arms of dashing Bob Taylor!

ROBERT
TAYLOR
HEDY
LAMARR
LADY of the
TROPICS

RIVOLI
NOW

HELD OVER
But Hurry, it stays for
only a few days ! !

25¢
to 5

GINGER ROGERS
DAVID NIVEN
in
"Bachelor
Mother"
Its Companion Picture
AND "Frontier Marshal"
with Randolph Scott
Nancy Kelly
★

HONOLULU

TODAY: Bigger . . . Better . . . Faster Than "Broadway Melody" or "Rosalie" . . . A SINGING . . . LAUGHING . . . DANCING MUSICALULU!

SEE: THE MOST IMPRESSIVE DANCES EVER SHOWN ON THE SCREEN! EXECUTED WITH BARBARIC ABANDON TO TOM-TOM DRUMS!

Starring **ELEANOR POWELL**
ROBERT **YOUNG**
GEORGE **BURNS** · GRACIE **ALLEN**

Hundreds of lovely hula girls . . . scores of lilting songs . . . spectacle to make you marvel!

THEY'LL SLAY YOU WITH LAUGHS . . . in their fastest, funniest screen treat!

MARTHA **RAYE** · BOB **HOPE**
in
"NEVER SAY DIE"
with ANDY DEVINE
ALAN MOWBRAY
directed by ELLIOTT NUGENT
PARAMOUNT PICTURE

PLUS

JACK **BENNY**
JOAN **BENNETT**
in
"ARTISTS AND MODELS ABROAD"

Sonja **HENIE** in
EVERYTHING HAPPENS AT NIGHT
RAY **MILLAND** · ROBERT **CUMMINGS**

279

Saturday

THE MOST FAMOUS FUN-FEUD IN FILM HISTORY!

90 EXPLOSIVE LAUGH-DAFFY MINUTES WITH THE SCREEN'S MOST COMICAL COMBINATION!

W. C. FIELDS

You Can't Cheat an Honest Man

Edgar **BERGEN** and Charlie **McCARTHY**

"MORTIMER"

Constance Moore
Mary Forbes · Thurston
Hall · Princess Baba

CAPITOL
STARTS TODAY!

John Steinbeck's
"OF MICE AND MEN"

BURGESS MEREDITH · BETTY FIELD · LON CHANEY Jr.

2nd Feature
James **STEWART**
Margaret **SULLAVAN**
"The SHOP AROUND THE CORNER"

TOMORROW!

Mighty Thrills

WITH THE SCREEN'S MOST ROMANTIC ADVENTURER!

Love and danger — the two strongest challenges to a soldier's heart! With the savage rhythm of jungle drums beating in his brain, a devil-may-care soldier faces the crises of his life beside the girl he loves.

ALWAYS OUTNUMBERED NEVER OUTFOUGHT

SAMUEL GOLDWYN presents

Gary **COOPER**

in

THE REAL GLORY

with

ANDREA LEEDS
DAVID NIVEN
REGINALD OWEN

RELEASED THRU UNITED ARTISTS

STARTS
TOMORROW ★ **CLASHING BLADES AND LOVABLE MAIDS!
RINGING TUNES AND BALMY BUFFOONS!**

D'ARTAGNAN RIDES AND
FIGHTS AND LOVES AGAIN!

A song on his lips....
romance in his heart....
and the Ritzes in his hair!

DON AMECHE
and
THE RITZ BROTHERS
in
A Musical Comedy Version of
ALEXANDRE DUMAS'

THE THREE
MUSKETEERS

with

**BINNIE BARNES • LIONEL ATWILL
GLORIA STUART • PAULINE MOORE
JOSEPH SCHILDKRAUT**
JOHN CARRADINE • MILES MANDER
DOUGLAS DUMBRILLE • JOHN KING

Directed by Allan Dwan
Associate Producer Raymond Griffith • Screen Play by
M. M. Musselman, William A. Drake and Sam Hellman
Special material by Sid Kuller and Ray Golden
A 20th Century-Fox Picture
Darryl F. Zanuck In Charge of Production

Swordplay! Horseplay!
With the Ritzes as
phoney Musketeers
more at home with a
carving knife than a
sword!

Hear:
"Song of the
Musketeers"
"My Lady"
"Voila"
by Samuel Pokrass
and Walter Bullock

—— EXTRA! ——
LATEST ISSUE
"MARCH of TIME"
featuring the story behind the
BOY SCOUT MOVEMENT

CAPITOL Starts TODAY!
JAMES CAGNEY
PAT O'BRIEN
GEORGE BRENT
"THE FIGHTING 69TH"
2nd FEATURE!
"CONGO MAISIE"
with ANN SOTHERN
John CARROLL

WINTER GARDEN Starts TODAY!
EDWARD G. ROBINSON
in "THE STORY OF DR. EHRLICH'S MAGIC BULLET"
RUTH GORDON • OTTO KRUGER • DONALD CRISP
Extra! DONALD DUCK AND
Joel McCREA • Nancy KELLY in "HE MARRIED HIS WIFE"

GINGER ROGERS
DAVID NIVEN
in
BACHELOR
MOTHER
with
CHARLES COBURN
FRANK ALBERTSON

WHAT A PICTURE!
The screen's big hit comedy! Ginger as a shopgirl foster-mother David as the boss' son.
HOW YOU'LL LAUGH!

ROBERT
DONAT
in
GOODBYE
MR. CHIPS
with GREER GARSON

The best picture of any year!

STARTS TODAY!

DRAMA
UNPARALLELED!
SPECTACLE
BEYOND BELIEF!!
The strangest, most colorful story ever told . . . relived on a stage as vast as life itself! Fifteen climactic sequences, over 3500 players . . . two hours of unbroken thrills and wonders in the picture you must say you've seen !!!

Charles LAUGHTON
in
"THE HUNCHBACK OF NOTRE DAME"
with
MAUREEN O'HARA
Sir CEDRIC HARDWICKE
THOMAS MITCHELL
And a Cast of Thousands!
RKO-Radio's $2,500,000 TRIUMPH!

ADDED!!
Walt Disney's all-color "OFFICER DUCK"
—and—
"WINTER PLAYGROUND"
World famous Skiers in action!

PARAMOUNT

CIRCLE
TODAY & TOMORROW

Thrill
Packed
Drama
Below
the
Border

Adolph Zukor presents

CLARENCE E. MULFORD'S

"IN OLD MEXICO"

featuring

WILLIAM BOYD

A Paramount Picture · a HARRY SHERMAN Production

CAPITOL
Starts TODAY

NORMA
SHEARER
Clark
GABLE
in
Clarence
BROWN'S production
Idiot's Delight

CAPITOL
STARTS TODAY!
ON THE SCREEN

GREAT
STARS!
ERROL FLYNN
BETTE DAVIS

GREAT
ROMANCE!

GREAT
NOVEL!
THE
SISTERS

plus

STAN OLIVER
LAUREL · HARDY
BLOCK-HEADS
A METRO-GOLDWYN-MAYER PICTURE

The Hardys ARRIVE TODAY!

IN THE NEWEST
AND GREATEST
OF THEIR HIT
PARADE!

IT'S HARDY FAMILY FUN AGAIN!

Hilarious . . . . as Andy struts in his topper and "Tux"
. . . and dates a cabaret glamour girl. . . . Love finds
Aunt Milly. . . . Marion knocks the stores for a row of
charge accounts. . . . Mom settles for a new frying pan.
. . . Pop winds up with a silk hat and all the bills. AND
YOU'LL HAVE THE TIME OF YOUR LIFE!

"The HARDYS RIDE HIGH"

WITH

MICKEY ROONEY
LEWIS STONE
CECILIA PARKER
FAY HOLDEN
ANN RUTHERFORD

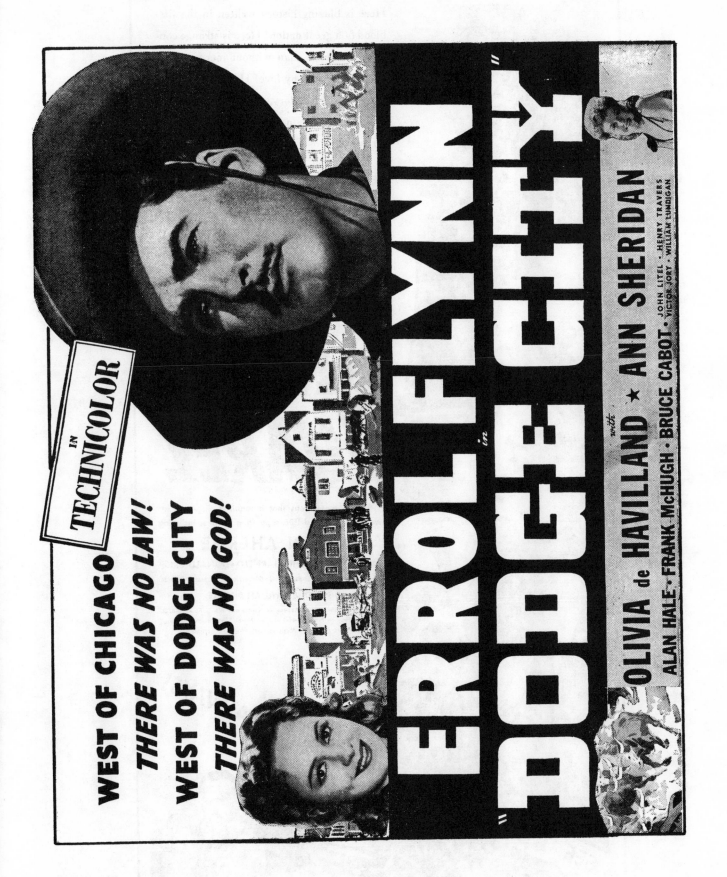

289

1940

Bing Crosby was now one of the top box office stars at Paramount Pictures. Pat O'Brien appeared in his great role as Knute Rockne, while Metro-Goldwyn-Mayer released two films depicting the life of Thomas Edison, with Mickey Rooney as *Young Tom Edison* and Spencer Tracy as *Edison The Man*. W. C. Fields made his famous comedy *The Bank Dick,* which is still being shown today. Gary Cooper starred in Samuel Goldwyn's austere film *The Westerner,* with Walter Brennan in his Academy Award winning role of Judge Roy Bean. Silent screen star Tom Mix was killed in an automobile accident in Arizona on October 12, 1940.

IT'S ONE LONG, LOUD L-A-U-G-H!

★ **TODAY!** ★

THAT INCOMPARABLE PAIR ARE BACK...ROWDILY ROMANCING...IN MOST FROTHY, ZIPPY, MARITAL MIXUP OF THE YEAR!

BILL WAKES UP WITH $147,000 AND A WIFE . . . AND HASN'T THE LEAST IDEA WHERE HE GOT EITHER OF THEM . . . IT'S RIOTOUS! . . . IT'S MAD! . . . YOU'RE IN FOR THE HOWL OF YOUR LIFE!

William **Powell** and **Myrna Loy** in *I LOVE YOU AGAIN*

with FRANK McHUGH · EDMUND LOWE

A METRO-GOLDWYN-MAYER HIT!

ORPHEUM

JUNGLE THRILLS
LOVE THRILLS
NOW

**DOUGLAS FAIRBANKS, Jr.
Madeleine CARROLL**

IN PARAMOUNT'S THRILLER

"SAFARI"

WITH
Lynne Overman • Billy Gilbert
Tullio Carminati

A RECKLESS ADVENTURER

. . . the sword-skilled Son of
Monte Cristo, fighting and
loving in the tradition of
his valiant, romantic name!

Edward Small presents

**THE SON of
MONTE
CRISTO**

starring

**LOUIS HAYWARD
JOAN BENNETT**

with

GEORGE SANDERS
FLORENCE BATES • MONTAGUE LOVE
screenplay by GEORGE BRUCE
directed by ROWLAND V. LEE
a ROWLAND V. LEE production
released thru UNITED ARTISTS

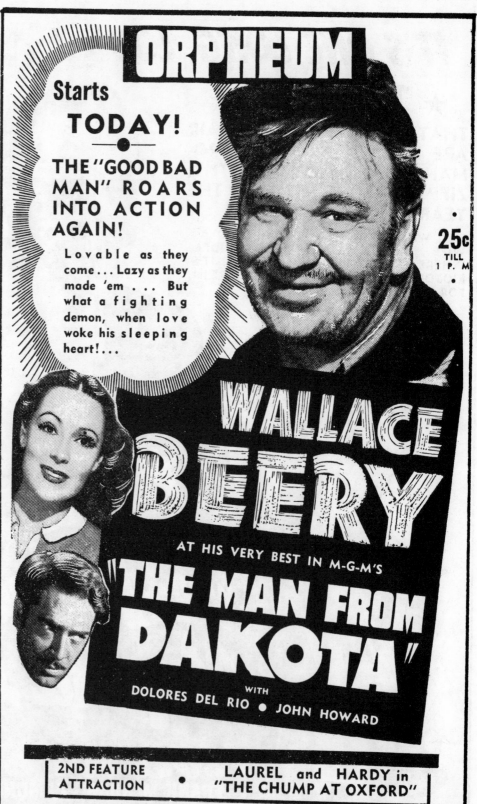

ORPHEUM

Starts
TODAY!

THE "GOOD BAD
MAN" ROARS
INTO ACTION
AGAIN!

Lovable as they
come . . . Lazy as they
made 'em . . . But
what a fighting
demon, when love
woke his sleeping
heart! . . .

25c
TILL
1 P.M

**WALLACE
BEERY**

AT HIS VERY BEST IN M-G-M'S

**"THE MAN FROM
DAKOTA"**

WITH
DOLORES DEL RIO • JOHN HOWARD

2ND FEATURE
ATTRACTION • LAUREL and HARDY in
"THE CHUMP AT OXFORD"

A Rootin', Tootin', Shootin' Riot of Laughs, Fun, Gags, Guns and Girls ... You'll Die Laughing at Rochester and his new girl friend!

PARAMOUNT'S BIG SPRING ROUND-UP OF REVELRY, RHYTHM AND ROMANCE

JACK *Buck* BENNY

AND HIS MAN FRIDAY

"ROCHESTER"

—in—

"BUCK BENNY RIDES AGAIN"

—with—

ANDY DEVINE — ELLEN DREW

PHIL HARRIS and HIS ORCHESTRA

DENNIS DAY

DON'T COME ALONE! You'll be Scared!.. OR CAN YOU TAKE IT?

DOUBLE WEIRD-MYSTERY SHOW

At his Fiendish Best in a THRILL PACKED Tale of Horror!

KARLOFF THE MAN WITH NINE LIVES

Roger PRYOR · Jo Ann SAYERS
Stanley BROWN
A COLUMBIA PICTURE

Plus Second THRILL-HIT!

He killed men slowly ... inch by inch!.. He Broke women's hearts piece by piece!

PETER LORRE ISLAND OF DOOMED MEN

with ROCHELLE HUDSON · ROBERT WILCOX
A COLUMBIA PICTURE

PALOMAR

THE LAUGHS
COMMENCE
TOMORROW!
WE PROMISE YOU
CONVULSIONS!

EDWARD G.
ROBINSON
IN HIS BULLET-PROOF PEST!

"Brother
Orchid"

AND
Teddy
THE
ROUGH
RIDER
Filmed
in
color!

with
ANN
SOTHERN
HUMPHREY
BOGART
DONALD CRISP
Ralph Bellamy
ALLEN JENKINS
A WARNER BROS. Picture

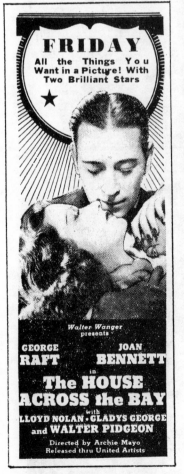

FRIDAY
All the Things You
Want in a Picture! With
Two Brilliant Stars

Walter Wanger
presents

GEORGE   JOAN
RAFT   BENNETT
in
The HOUSE
ACROSS the BAY
with
LLOYD NOLAN · GLADYS GEORGE
and WALTER PIDGEON
Directed by Archie Mayo
Released thru United Artists

CAGNEY!
SHERIDAN!
O'BRIEN!

Terrific!
in

TORRID
ZONE

with ANDY (Hi'ya Buck!) DEVINE
HELEN VINSON · Directed by WM. KEIGHLEY
IT'S A NEW WARNER BROS. SUCCESS

295

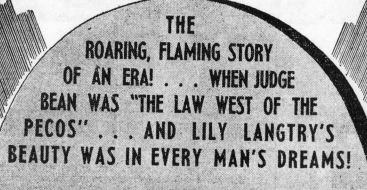

THE
ROARING, FLAMING STORY
OF AN ERA! . . . WHEN JUDGE
BEAN WAS "THE LAW WEST OF THE
PECOS" . . . AND LILY LANGTRY'S
BEAUTY WAS IN EVERY MAN'S DREAMS!

SAMUEL GOLDWYN presents

Gary COOPER

in "THE
WESTERNER"

with WALTER BRENNAN
DORIS DAVENPORT
FRED STONE

RELEASED THRU
UNITED ARTISTS

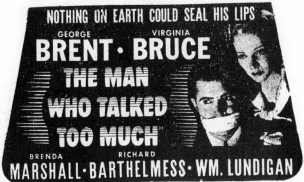

NOTHING ON EARTH COULD SEAL HIS LIPS

GEORGE VIRGINIA
BRENT · BRUCE

THE MAN
WHO TALKED
TOO MUCH

BRENDA RICHARD
MARSHALL · BARTHELMESS · WM. LUNDIGAN

SHE WAS SO
DARNED
ALLURING
AND HE HAD
THAT GLEAM
IN HIS EYE!

*Meet the
Merriest
Mad Man
That Ever
Barged
Into a
Lady's
Boudoir!*

Loretta
YOUNG
MET
Melvyn
DOUGLAS
AND—

★ **He Stayed for
Breakfast** ★

with
Alan MARSHAL
Eugene PALLETTE
Una O'CONNOR

A Columbia
Production

HELD
OVER

FOR A
FEW DAYS
MORE
•
What Ever You
Do, Don't Miss
"Lillian Russell"

YOU'LL LOVE IT!
Here is a "honey" of a picture.
Full of romance, comedy and
thrilling climaxes that's even
greater than "Alexander's Rag-
time Band."

"LILLIAN
RUSSELL"
with
ALICE FAYE
DON AMECHE
HENRY FONDA
EDWARD ARNOLD

A 20th Century-Fox Picture

25¢
TILL
1 P.M.

EXTRA!
SELECTED
SHORT
SUBJECTS

JAMES
STEWART
(That guy from Washington)
ROSALIND
RUSSELL
(That woman from 'The Women')
IN THE COMEDY ROMANCE
OF THE SEASON!
"No time for comedy"

Meet THE HOWARDS OF VIRGINIA

Thrill as their romance flowers!

CARY GRANT
MARTHA SCOTT
THE HOWARDS OF VIRGINIA

STARTS TODAY!

MICKEY
ROONEY
AS
"YOUNG TOM EDISON"
with Fay BAINTER

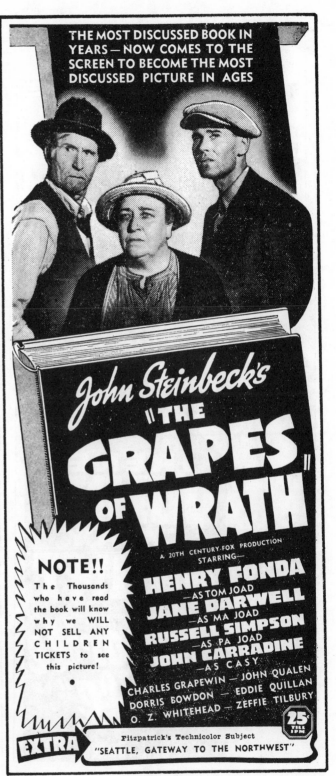

THE MOST DISCUSSED BOOK IN YEARS — NOW COMES TO THE SCREEN TO BECOME THE MOST DISCUSSED PICTURE IN AGES

John Steinbeck's
"THE
GRAPES
OF WRATH"

A 20TH CENTURY-FOX PRODUCTION
STARRING—

HENRY FONDA
—AS TOM JOAD
JANE DARWELL
—AS MA JOAD
RUSSELL SIMPSON
—AS PA JOAD
JOHN CARRADINE
—AS CASY

CHARLES GRAPEWIN — JOHN QUALEN
DORRIS BOWDON — EDDIE QUILLAN
O. Z. WHITEHEAD — ZEFFIE TILBURY

NOTE!!
The Thousands who have read the book will know why we WILL NOT SELL ANY CHILDREN TICKETS to see this picture!

25¢ TILL 1PM

EXTRA

Fitzpatrick's Technicolor Subject
"SEATTLE, GATEWAY TO THE NORTHWEST"

HOWLS GALORE! . . . WHEN OUR DEFECTIVE
DETECTIVE BECOMES A FIRST NATIONAL HERO
THROUGH NO VAULT OF HIS OWN!

W.C. FIELDS

in THE

Bank Dick

with UNA MERKEL
RICHARD PURCELL
FRANKLIN PANGBORN

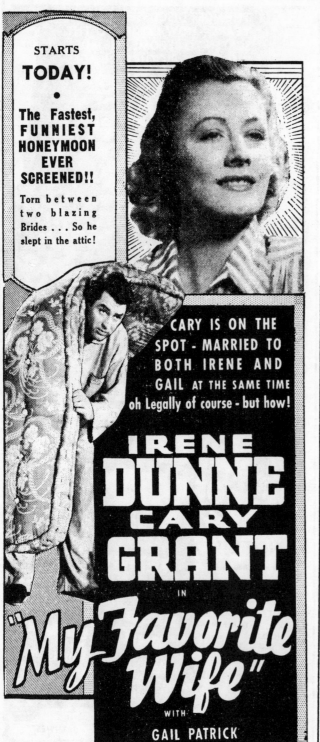

STARTS
TODAY!
•
The Fastest,
FUNNIEST
HONEYMOON
EVER
SCREENED!!

Torn between
two blazing
Brides . . . So he
slept in the attic!

CARY IS ON THE
SPOT - MARRIED TO
BOTH IRENE AND
GAIL AT THE SAME TIME
oh Legally of course - but how!

IRENE
DUNNE
CARY
GRANT

in

"My Favorite Wife"

WITH
GAIL PATRICK

ORPHEUM

NOW! BREAKING ALL RECORDS!!

Radio's top comics bring their famous feud
to the screen in the merriest holiday show
you've ever seen!!!

JACK   FRED
BENNY ★ ALLEN
"LOVE THY
NEIGHBOR"
...MARY MARTIN and ROCHESTER

And—its companion picture
GENE STRATTON "LADDIE"
PORTER'S

STARTS TODAY!

...At Last the Screen Brings You the Mightiest Adventure Romance of All Time!!!

●

The roaring magnificence of "Union Pacific"...the pulse-pounding action of "The Plainsman"...two surging love stories woven into an unforgettable drama of human emotions...told against the blazing beauty of the northern forests...filmed in SUPER TECHNICOLOR!

Cecil B. DeMILLE'S

NORTH WEST MOUNTED POLICE

with

GARY COOPER
PAULETTE GODDARD
MADELEINE CARROLL
Robert PRESTON • Preston FOSTER
Lynne Overman • Akim Tamiroff • George Bancroft • Lon Chaney Jr. • Walter Hampden

A Paramount Production

Starts TODAY! **COLONIAL**
The Greatest **HORROR SHOW** of all time!

Boris **KARLOFF**
Bela **LUGOSI**
BLACK FRIDAY

Nathaniel Hawthorne's
The HOUSE OF THE SEVEN GABLES
George Sanders

TWO BIG HITS!

THE SCREEN'S GREATEST STAR IN HIS GREATEST SCREEN TRIUMPH

SPENCER TRACY

IN M-G-M'S NEW SENSATION

"EDISON THE MAN"

WITH
RITA JOHNSON
LYNN OVERMAN
CHARLES COBURN
GENE LOCKHART

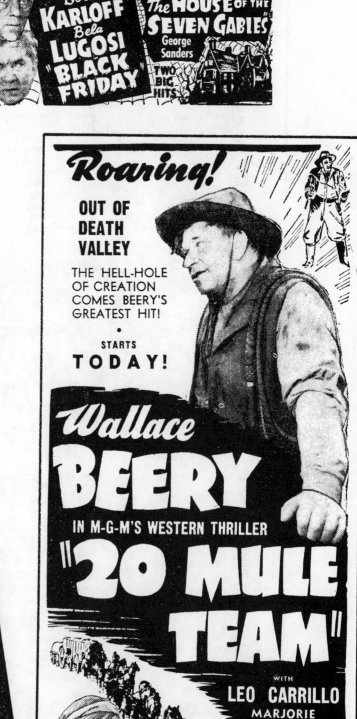

Roaring!

OUT OF DEATH VALLEY

THE HELL-HOLE OF CREATION COMES BEERY'S GREATEST HIT!

STARTS **TODAY!**

Wallace BEERY

IN M-G-M'S WESTERN THRILLER

"20 MULE TEAM"

WITH
LEO CARRILLO
MARJORIE RAMBEAU